1971

the portico
of the mystery
of the second virtue

by

Charles Péguy

Translated by

Dorothy Brown Aspinwall

The Scarecrow Press, Inc.

Metuchen, N.J.   1970

Translator's Preface

The title of this poem states its theme and modestly limits
its scope: it is the portico, the entrance porch, the approach, the
introduction to the mystery of the second virtue, hope. Theological-
ly, a mystery is a religious truth that is usually beyond human reason; in this poem the mystery of hope is difficult to understand even
for God who marvels that men continue to hope despite all the bad
days that are rained upon them. The whole poem is a monologue
in which God speaks through the voice of Madame Gervaise, a young
nun whom Péguy had introduced in The Mystery of the Charity of
Joan of Arc (1910).

Who is this Charles Péguy who writes speeches for God? A
French peasant born at the edge of Orleans on January 7, 1873, an
ardent young revolutionary socialist, a lifelong devotee of Joan of
Arc, a bitter polemicist, initiator, editor, proofreader, and publisher
of the series of books called Cahiers de la Quinzaine (of which this
Mystery is Series XIII, Number 4), prolific author of political prose
and religious verse, altruistic defender of Dreyfus and of Bergson,
prodigal son who returned to the faith but whose children were un-
baptized at the time of his death and who may never have heard
mass in his adult life, enthusiastic infantry officer who was killed
by a German bullet on September 5, 1914, in the war which he
truly believed would make possible a new era of peace, freedom,
and equality.

Who was Charles Péguy? In 1914 he was overshadowed by
Maurice Barrès, Charles Maurras, Paul Claudel, Romain Rolland;
beyond his circle of patient friends and staunch enemies, he was
little read. Today he is recognized as one of the great original
poets of France. Of the eight hundred copies of his first Joan of
Arc printed in 1897 one copy sold; The portico of the mystery of
the second virtue has run to sixty-six editions in France.

Péguy's style is like that of no other poet: his _portico_ is written in language that any French child or peasant could understand and in free verse with, usually, a period at the end of the line. These full stops, that frequently disregard syntax, are designed to slow the reader and to force him to meditate, as are the blank spaces of varying size that occur at irregular intervals between lines of verse. But the most strikingly original feature of Péguy's style is the constant repetition by which he establishes a rhythm that carries the reader along relentlessly. This is not just the simple repetition of a word or phrase; it is the repetition again and again of a thought with each repetition resuming the thought and adding one more element. Péguy builds up his exposition in the same way that waves of an incoming tide wash up the beach with each wave repeating the action of the wave before yet reaching just a little more of the dry sand.

While it is, indeed, thoughts, ideas, that interest Péguy, the _portico_ is no abstruse metaphysical treatise. Theological concepts are reduced to humble, humanly comprehensible dimensions. Hope is a little girl skipping along between her two big sisters, Faith and Charity. God suggests wryly to sleepless worriers that those who do sleep and leave their affairs in His hands during the night often find things none the worse in the morning.

The whole poem is an affirmation of God's interest in His world, and an explanation of the Christian's rôle in the design of creation.

(Madame Gervaise enters.)

Madame Gervaise

The faith that I love best, said God, is hope.

Faith does not surprise me.

It is not surprising.

I burst forth so strikingly in my creation.

In the sun and the moon and the stars.

In all my creatures.

In the stars of the firmament and the fish of the sea.

In the universe of my creatures.

On the face of the earth and the face of the waters.

In the movements of the stars in the sky.

In the wind that blows over the sea and the wind that blows
down the valley.

In the calm valley.

In the secluded valley.

In plants and animals and the beasts of the forest.

And in man.

My creature.

In peoples and men and in kings and common people.

In man and in woman his mate.

And especially in children.

My creatures.

In the gaze and the voices of children.

For children are more truly my creatures.

Than men.

They have not yet been distorted by life.

On earth.

And beyond all others they are my servants.

Before all.

5

And the voices of children are purer than the voice of the wind
in the calm of the valley.
In the secluded valley.
And the gaze of children is purer than the blue of the sky,
than the milky sky, purer than a star's ray in the calm
night.
Yes, I burst forth so strikingly in my creation.
On the face of the mountains and the face of the plain.
In bread and wine and in the man who plows and the man who sows,
in the harvest of grain and the harvest of grapes.
In light and in shadows.
And in the heart of man, which is the deepest thing in the world.
In the created world.
So deep that it is impenetrable to every gaze.
Excepting my gaze.
In the tempest that stirs waves and the tempest that stirs leaves.
On the trees in the forest.
And conversely in the calm of a beautiful evening.
In the sand of the sea and in the stars which are grains of
sand in the sky.
In the stone of the threshold and the stone of the hearth and
the stone of the altar.
In prayer and in the sacraments.
In the houses of men and in the church which is my house on
earth.
In my creature the eagle which flies among summits.
The royal eagle which has a wing-spread of two meters and
perhaps three.
And in my creature the ant that crawls and hoards minutely.
In the earth.
In the ant my servant.
And even in the serpent.
In the ant my servant, my tiny servant that hoards minutely,
the miser.
That works like a wretch and does not stop and takes no rest.
But death and the long sleep of winter.

6

(shrugging his shoulders at so much evidence
in the face of so much evidence.)

I burst forth so strikingly in my whole creation.

In my tiny tiny creature, in my tiny servant, in the tiny ant.

That hoards minutely, like man.

Like tiny man.

And that hollows tunnels in the earth.

In the cellars of the earth.

For storing his paltry treasures.

Wretched treasures.

And even in the serpent.

Which deceived woman and because of that crawls on its belly.

And which is my creature and my servant.

The serpent which deceived woman.

My maidservant.

Which deceived man my servant.

I burst forth so strikingly in my creation.

In everything that happens to man, to peoples, and to the poor.

And even to the rich.

Who do not wish to be my creatures.

And who shield themselves

From being my servants.

In all the evil and good things man makes and destroys.

(And I let it go, because I am the master and I make what he
    has destroyed and I destroy what he has made.)

Even to the temptation of sin.

Even there.

And in everything that happened to my son.

Because of man.

My creature.

Whom I had created.

In the conception, the birth and the life and the death of my
    son.

And in the holy sacrifice of the mass.

In every birth and every life.
And in every death.
And in the life eternal which will never end.
Which will overcome death.

I burst forth so strikingly in my creation.

That truly these poor people would have to be blind not to
see me.

Charity, said God, does not surprise me.
It is not surprising.
These poor creatures are so wretched that unless they have
hearts of stone, why would they not love each other.
Why would they not love their brothers.
Why would they not take the bread from their own mouths, their
daily bread, to give it to wretched passing children.
My son received from them just such charity.
My son their brother.
Such great charity.
Hope, said God, that does surprise me.
Even me.
That is surprising.

That these poor children seeing all that goes on should believe
that tomorrow will be better.
That they see what goes on today and believe that tomorrow
morning will be better.
That is surprising and it is certainly the greatest wonder of
our grace.
I myself am surprised at it.
And my grace must indeed be of incredible power.
And flow from a spring like an endless river.
Since that first time it flowed and during the eternity it has
been flowing.

In the natural and supernatural creation.

In my creation spiritual and carnal and yet spiritual.

In my creation eternal and temporal and yet eternal.

Mortal and immortal.

And that time, oh that time, since that time that it flowed,
   like a river of blood, from the pierced side of my son.

How great must be my grace, and the power of my grace if this
   little hope, wavering at the breath of sin, trembling in
   every breeze, nervous at the least breath,

is as unchangeable, remains as faithful, as upright, as pure;
   and invincible, and immortal, and impossible to quench; as
   this little flame in the sanctuary.

Which burns forever in the faithful lamp.

A flickering flame has traversed the denseness of worlds.

A wavering flame has traversed the denseness of time.

A nervous flame has traversed the denseness of nights.

Since that first time when my grace flowed for the creation
   of the world.

Since the eternity that my grace has been flowing for the pre-
   servation of the world.

Since that time when the blood of my son flowed for the redemption of the world.

A flame impossible to assail, impossible to quench by the breath
   of death.

What surprises me, said God, is hope.

And I cannot get over it.

This little hope who looks like a slip of a girl.

This little girl hope.

Immortal hope.

For my three virtues, said God.

The three virtues my creatures.

My daughters my children.

Are themselves like my other creatures.

Of the race of men.

Faith is a loyal Wife.

Charity is a Mother.

A loving mother, all heart.

Or an elder sister who is like a mother.

Hope is a little slip of a girl.

Who came into the world on Christmas day last year.

Who is still playing with a snowman.

With her little fir trees of German wood covered with painted frost.

And with her ox and ass of painted wood

From Germany.

And with her crib full of straw that the beasts do not eat.

Because they are made of wood.

Yet it is this little girl who will traverse the worlds.

This little slip of a girl.

She alone, bearing the others, who will traverse the consummated worlds.

As the star led the three kings from the farthest Orient.

Toward the cradle of my son.

So she a wavering flame

Alone will lead the Virtues and the Worlds.

A flame will pierce the everlasting shadows.

The priest speaks.

Minister of God the priest says:

What are the three theological virtues?

The child replies:

The three theological virtues are Faith, Hope and Charity.

Why are Faith, Hope and Charity called theological virtues?

Faith, Hope and Charity are called theological virtues because
  they refer directly to God.

What is Hope?

Hope is a supernatural virtue by which we confidently expect
  from God his grace in this world and eternal glory in the
  next.

Make an act of Hope.

O my God, I hope, with firm confidence, that you will give me,
  through the merits of Jesus Christ, your grace in this world,
  your glory in the next, because you have promised me this,
  and you are supremely faithful to your promises.

We too often forget, my child, that hope is a virtue, that it
  is a theological virtue, and that of all the virtues, and
  of the three theological virtues, it is perhaps the most
  pleasing to God.
  That it is assuredly the most difficult, that it is perhaps
  the only difficult virtue, and that doubtless it is the most
  pleasing to God.

Faith can be taken for granted.   Faith gets along on its own.
  In order to believe one need only let go, look about.   In
  order not to believe one would have to make a violent effort,
  to torture, to torment, thwart oneself.   To brace oneself.
  Attack backwards, reverse oneself, increase one's strength.
  Faith is quite natural, quite lively, quite simple, quite
  thriving.   Heartily thriving.   Very lively.   It is a good
  woman of one's acquaintance, a good old woman, a good old

parishioner, a good old woman of the parish, an old grand-
mother, a good parishioner. She tells us stories of olden
times, that happened in olden times.

In order not to believe, my child, one would have to close his
eyes and stop up his ears. So as not to see, so as not to
believe.

Charity unfortunately is taken for granted. Charity gets along
on its own. To love one's neighbor, one has only to let
oneself go, to look at so much distress. In order not to
love one's neighbor one would have to make a violent effort,
to torture, torment, thwart oneself. Harm oneself. Go
against nature, attack backwards, reverse oneself. Increase
one's strength. Charity is quite natural, quite spontaneous,
quite simple, heartily thriving. It is the first impulse
of the heart. It is the first impulse which is best.
Charity is a mother and a sister.

In order not to love one's neighbor, my child, one would have
to close his eyes and stop up his ears.
To so many cries of distress.

But hope is not taken for granted. Hope does not get along on
its own. To hope, my child, one must be very happy, one
must have obtained, received great grace.

It is faith that is easy and not believing that would be impossible. It is charity that is easy and not loving that would
be impossible. But it is hoping that is difficult.

(in a low voice shamefacedly.)

12

And the easy way and the inclination is toward despair and that
  is the great temptation.

Little hope moves forward between her two big sisters and is
  not even noticed.
On the road to salvation, on the carnal road, on the rough
  road to salvation, on the endless road, on the road between
  her two sisters little hope
Moves forward.
Between her two big sisters.
The one who is married.
And the one who is a mother.
And all the attention, all the attention of Christian people
  is given to the two big sisters.
The first and the last.
Who attend to the most pressing things first.
To the present time.
To the fleeting moment that passes.
Christian people see only the two big sisters, pay attention
  only to the two big sisters.
The one on the right and the one on the left.
And they practically do not see the one in the middle.
The little one, who still goes to school.
And who walks.
Hidden in the skirts of her sisters.
And they willingly believe that it is the two big sisters who
  are pulling the little one along by the hand.
In the middle.
Between the two of them.
To make her walk this rough road to salvation.
They are blind not to see on the contrary.
That it is the one in the middle who is pulling her big sisters.
And that without her they would be nothing.
But two women already old.
Two middle-aged women.

Worn by life.

It is she, the little one, who pulls the whole weight.
For Faith sees only what is.
But she, she alone, sees what will be.
Charity loves only what is.
But she, she alone, loves what will be.

Faith sees what is.
In Time and in Eternity.
Hope sees what will be.
In time and for eternity.
In the future of eternity so to speak.

Charity loves what is.
In Time and in Eternity.
God and her neighbor.
As Faith sees.
God and creation.
But Hope loves what will be.
In time and for eternity.

In the future of eternity so to speak.

Hope sees what as yet is not and will be.
She loves what as yet is not and will be
In the future of time and eternity.

On the sandy, toilsome, uphill road.
The uphill way.

Pulled, dragging on the arms of her two big sisters,
Who hold her by the hand,
Little hope
Moves forward.
And in the middle between her two big sisters she seems to be
   letting herself be pulled
Like a child who has not the strength to walk.
And is pulled along the road in spite of herself.
And in reality it is she who leads the other two.
And pulls them.
And who leads everybody.
And pulls everybody,
For people never work except for their children.

And the two big sisters walk only for the sake of the little one.

My three virtues, said God.
Master of the Three Virtues.
My three virtues are no different from men and women in their
   homes.
It is not the children who work.
For people never work except for their children.
It is not the child who goes to the fields, who plows and sows,
   and reaps the grain and gathers the grapes and who prunes
   the vines and fells the trees and saws the wood.
For winter.
To warm the house in winter.
What father would have the heart to work except for his children.
If it were not for the sake of his children.
And in winter when he works hard.
In the forest.
When he works the hardest.
With the bush-hook and saw and the hatchet and axe.
In the icy forest.

In winter when snakes sleep in the woods because they are frozen.

And when the bitter north wind blows.

Piercing his bones.

Biting through all his limbs.

And he is thoroughly chilled and his teeth chatter.

And the frost forms icicles in his beard.

Suddenly he thinks of his wife who has stayed at home.

Of his wife who is such a good housewife.

Whose husband he is in the sight of God.

And of his children who are comfortable at home.

Who are playing and enjoying themselves right now by the hearth.

And are perhaps wrestling

Together.

For fun.

They pass before his eyes, in a flash before his mind's eye,
    before his soul's eye.

They live in his memory and his heart and his soul and his
    soul's eye.

They live in his gaze.

In a flash he sees his three children playing and laughing by
    the hearth.

His three children, two boys and a girl.

Whose father he is in the sight of God.

His eldest, his boy, who was twelve in the month of September.

His daughter who was nine in the month of September.

And his youngest who was seven in the month of June.

So the girl is in the middle.

As is proper.

So that she may be defended by her two brothers.

In life.

One before and one after.

His three children who will succeed and survive him.

On earth.

Who will have his house and his land.

And if he has neither house nor land who will have at least
    his tools.

(If he has neither house nor land they will not have any either.
That is all there is to it.)
(He managed to live without them.
They will do as he did.   They will work.)
His axe and his hatchet his bush-hook and his saw.
And his hammer and file.
And his bucket and pick.
And his spade for spading the earth.
And if he has neither house nor land.
At least they will inherit his tools.
His good tools.
Which have so often served him.
Which are worn to his grasp.
Which have so many times spaded the same earth.
His tools, in constant use, have made his hand horny and gleaming.
But he, by use, has made the handles of his tools polished and
    gleaming.
And from work his skin has become as hard and as tanned as the
    handles of his tools.
Through the handles of his tools his sons will find, his sons
    will inherit the hardness of his hands.
But also their skill, their great skill.
For he is a good plowman and a good wooodcutter.
And a good vine-grower.
And with his tools his sons will inherit, his children will
    inherit.
What he has given them, what nobody could take from them.
(Almost not even God.)
(So much has God given to man.)
The strength of his race, the strength of his blood.
For they are his descendents.
And they are French and Lorrainese.
Sons of good strain and of good family.
And blood will tell.
Sons of a good mother.

17

And above all, away above all, along with his tools and his strain
and his blood his children will inherit.
That which is worth more than a house and a parcel of land to
leave to one's children.
For the house and the land are perishable and will perish.
And the house and the land are exposed to the wind of winter.
To the bitter north wind that blows in this forest.
But the blessing of God is not blown away by any wind.
That which is worth more than tools, which is more workable,
more practical than tools.
That which does more work than tools.
And anyway tools finally wear out.
Like men.
That which is worth more, which is more lasting than strain
and blood.
Even more lasting.
For even strain and blood are perishable and will perish.
Except the blood of Jesus.
Which will be shed world without end.
And even strain and blood are exposed to the wind of winter.
And there can be a winter of the strain.
Along with his house perhaps if he has one and his land.
With his tools certainly and his strain and his blood his child-
ren will inherit.
That which is above all.
The blessing of God which is on his house and on his strain.
The grace of God which is more valuable than anything.
He knows this.
The grace which is given to the poor man and to him who works.
And who brings up his children well.
He knows this.
Because God has promised it.
And he is supremely faithful to his promises.

His three children who are growing so big.

If only they do not get sick.
And who will surely be taller than he.
(How proud of this he is in his heart.)
And his two boys will be awfully strong.
His two boys will replace him, his children will take his place
    on earth.
When he is no longer here.
His place in the parish and his place in the forest.
His place in the church and his place in the house.
His place in the town and his place in the vineyard
And on the plain and on the hill and in the valley.
His place in Christendom. Well. Anyway.
His place as a man and a Christian.
His place as a parishioner, as a plowman.
His place as a peasant.
His place as a father.
His place as a son of Lorraine and a Frenchman.
For these are places, Heaven knows, that must be occupied.
And all that must go on.
When he is no longer here as at present.
In the same way if not better.
The peasantry must go on.
And the vines and the grain and the harvest and the gathering
    of grapes.
And the plowing of the earth.
And the pasturing of beasts.
When he is no longer here as at present.
In the same way if not better.
Christendom must go on.
The Church militant.
And for this there must be Christians.
Always.
The parish must go on.
France must go on and Lorraine.
Long after he has ceased to be.

As well as at present.

If not better.

He thinks tenderly of the time when he will have ceased to be
and when his children will take his place.

On earth.

In the sight of God.

Of that time when he will have ceased to be and when his children will be.

And when his name is spoken in the town, when he is talked of,
when his name comes up, by chance in conversation, it will
no longer be of him they are speaking but of his sons.

It will be both of him and not of him, since it will be of
his sons.

It will be his name and it will no longer be his name, since
it will have become the name of his sons.

And he is proud of it in his heart and how tenderly he thinks.

That he will no longer be himself but his sons.

And that his name will no longer be his name but the name of
his sons.

That his name will no longer serve him but will serve his sons.

Who will bear the name honorably in the sight of God.

Openly and proudly.

As he does.

Better than he does.

And when his name is spoken, it will be his son that is being
called, it is of his son that they will be speaking.

He himself will long have been in the cemetery.

Round about the church.

He, that is to say his body.

Side by side with his forefathers and the fathers of his forefathers.

In a row with them.

With his father and his grandfather whom he knew.

And with all the others all those that he has not known.

All the men and all the women of his strain.

All the ancient men and ancient women.
His ancestors and forebears.
And his gradmothers.
As many as there have been since the parish was founded.
By some saintly founder.
Come from Jesus.
His body, for as for his soul long ago
He commended it to God.
Putting it under the protection of his patron saints.

He will sleep, his body will rest thus.
Among his kin, (waiting for his kin).
Waiting for the resurrection of the body.
Until the resurrection of the body his body will rest thus.

He thinks tenderly of the time when he will no longer be needed.
And when all will go on just the same.
Because there will be others.
Who will bear the same burden.
And who perhaps, and who doubtless will bear it better.

He thinks tenderly of the time when he will have ceased to be.
Because it is true, isn't it, one cannot go on forever.
One cannot be and have been.
And when everything will go on just the same.
When everything will go on just as well.
On the contrary.
When everything can only go better.
On the contrary.
Because his children will be there, at this time.
His children will do better than he, of course.
And the world will be better run.
Later on.
He is not resentful of this.
On the contrary.
Nor of having come into the world at a difficult period.

And of having doubtless prepared maybe a less difficult period
   for his sons.
What madman would be resentful of his sons and of the sons of
   his sons.

Does he not work solely for his children.

He thinks tenderly of the time when people will scarcely think
   of him except on account of his children.
(If only they would think of him sometimes.   Occasionally.)
When his name will ring (cordially) in the town,
It will be a man calling his son Marcel or his son Pierre.
It will be a man needing his son Marcel or his son Pierre.
And he will call them, happy to see them.   And he will look
   for them.
For it is they who will reign with the men of their age and
   their period.
It is they who will reign on the face of the earth.
Perhaps for a little while longer some old man who remembers
Will say.
The two Sévin boys, they're fine fellows.
It is not surprising.
Look at the family.
Their father was such a fine man.
A little later young men will repeat with confidence:
Their father was such a fine man.
But already they will not know anything about it.
Then they will not know any more and even this, even this remark
   will be heard no more.
He thinks tenderly of the time when he will not even be a subject
   of conversation.
It is for this, for this that he works, for isn't it for their
   children that people work.

He will be only a body in six feet of earth under six feet of
   earth under a cross.

22

But his children will be.
He greets tenderly the new time when he will have ceased to be.
When he will be no more.
When his children will be.
The reign of his children.

He thinks tenderly of the period which will no longer be his
    period.
But the period of his children.
The reign (of time) of his children on earth.
In that time when people say the Sévins it will not be he but
    they.
Without any explanation.

His children will bear the name of Sévin.
(Or the name of Chénin, or Jouffin, or Damrémont or any other
    name of Lorraine.
Any other Christian surname belonging to France and Lorraine.)

At the thought of his children who will have become men and
    women.
At the thought of the period of his children, of the reign of
    his children.
On earth,
In their turn,
A tenderness, a warmth, a feeling of self-respect rises in him.
(Good heavens, could that be pride.
But God will forgive him.)
How well and strong his sons will be in the forest, great God.
Boys as strong as oaks.
In the forest when the winter wind blows.
The bitter north wind.
That will pierce their bones.
And make icicles in their beards.

He laughs at the thought of what they will look like.

He laughs to himself and perhaps even outwardly.

Openly.

When he thinks what they will look like when they have beards.

And he thinks tenderly of his daughter who will be such a good
    housewife.

Because surely she will be like her mother.

He will have ceased to be, of course he will have ceased to be.

He will have died.

But there will be others, good God there will be others,

One must hope,

Who already know the taste of bread and who will know how to
    bite into a good round loaf.

Who will hungrily eat

Their daily bread.

Who will hungrily eat their daily bread and their eternal bread.

(They will get along very well without him, and he will no
    longer sit at table, for it is crowded at the table when
    new children arrive and grow up.)

Others his children who will live and die after him if things
    follow their natural order.

And whom he will meet again in paradise.

There will be others, thank God:

France must continue.

France will not be idle, nor Christendom nor Lorraine.

And the parish will not be idle.

Nor will the vines nor the grain.

It is natural that a father die before his children.

He thinks of them, by God's grace, the blood at once flows back
    into his heart.

And warms him as much.

And surges back into all his limbs right to the tips of his
    fingers.

24

As much as if he had drunk a glass of good Meuse wine.
From the slopes above Cepoy.
And the numbness that he had in his fingers, (and it did not
    help to blow on his fingers).
Disappears as if by magic.
And now he feels nothing but the prickling of warmth at the
    tips of his fingers.
And the bitter north wind.
Which is still blowing.
Because it has no children.
Because it is a creature without life.
And does not know about all those things.
The bitter north wind in the forest.
Comes now and freezes two big tears that are foolishly running
    down his cheeks.
In the furrows of his two cheeks and disappearing in his
    bushy beard.
Like two icicles.
Then he, laughing and ashamed.
Laughing inwardly and ashamed inwardly and outwardly.
And even laughing aloud.
For he is gentle and ashamed of weeping.
In a man.
Then the poor man tries to be tricky.
Pretends he has not wept.
People always try to be tricky.
He looks around covertly to see if anyone is watching him.
If anyone has seen him.
By any chance.
Laughing inwardly and secretly in his beard.
He hurries to wipe the two tears from his cheek.
And to brush them away.
He swallows and passes his tongue over his lips.
At the corner of his lips the salt water of his tears.
That seep through his beard.
And so clumsily with his hand.

Awkwardly.

Slantingly.

Downwards at an angle.

With the back of his thumb he hurries to brush away his tears
   and the trace of his tears.

So that no one should notice.

So that no one should see that he has wept.

And go making fun of him in the town.

Because a man must not weep.

And his wife who stayed at home today.

But who usually goes to the fields too.

Who is such a good housewife.

And such a good Christian.

Would she have such will for the work.

And for the housework.

If she were not working for her children.

So and not otherwise everyone works for the little girl hope.

Everything we do is for the sake of our children.

And it is the children who are responsible for all that is done.

For all that we do.

As if they took us by the hand.

So that all that is done, all that everyone does is done for
   the little girl hope.

Everything small is the finest and the greatest of all.

Everything new is the finest and the greates of all.

And baptism is the sacrament of the little ones.

And baptism is the newest sacrament.

And baptism is consciousness just beginning.

Everything in its beginning has a virtue that is never regained.

A strength, a newness, a freshness like dawn.

A youthfulness, an ardor.

An enthusiasm.

A simplicity.

A dawning that is never regained.

The first day is the finest day.

The first day is perhaps the only fine day.

And baptism is the sacrament of the first day.

And baptism is all that is finest and greatest.

Excepting the sacrifice.

And the partaking of the body of our Lord.

In what is just beginning there is a source, a strain that is
    not repeated.

A start, a childhood that is not regained, that is never
    regained.

Now the little girl hope

Is she who is always beginning.

This dawning

Perpetual dawning.

This childhood

Perpetual childhood.   Good heavens, what would we do, what would
    we be, if it were not for children.   What would become of us.

And the two big sisters very well know that without her they
    would be only temporary maidservants.

Old maids in a thatched hut.

In a dilapidated shanty that gets more ramshackle every day.

That wears out along with the old women.

Who grow old all alone and who live drearily in a hovel.

Childless women.

A dying line.

But through her on the contrary they know that they are two

generous women.

Two women of promise.

Two women who have something to do in life.

And that through this little girl they are bringing up they
hold all time and eternity itself in the hollow of their
hands.

So it is the children who do nothing.

Ah the sly fellows who pretend to do nothing.

The rascals,

They know what they are doing,

The innocents.

Innocents want for nothing*

There is no mistake about it.

They know that they are responsible for everything; and more
than everything;

With their innocent looks;

With their appearance of knowing nothing;

Of not knowing;

Since it is for them that we work.

In reality.

Since it is only for them that we work.

And nothing is done but for them.

And everything that is done in the world is done only for them.

Which explains the look of confidence they have.

So pleasant to see.

The frank gaze, the gaze that cannot be met and yet meets all
others.

So gentle, so pleasant to see.

The gaze impossible to meet.

The frank gaze, the direct gaze they have, the gentle gaze,

---

* In French this is a proverb.

28

that comes direct from paradise.
So sweet to see, and to receive, the gaze of paradise.
Which explains the brows they have.
Their confident brows.
This flat, this bossed, this high, this square brow.
This confidence they have.
Which is the very confidence.
Of hope.

Their bossed brows, washed and clean from baptism.
From the waters of baptism.

And this manner of speech they have, these voices so gentle
and yet so confident.
So sweet to hear, so young.
These voices of paradise.
For their speech has a promise, a secret inward confidence.
As their young gaze has a promise, a secret inward promise,
and their brows and their whole persons.
Their little, majestic, reverend persons.

Happy children; happy father.
Happy hope.
Happy childhood. Their little bodies, their little persons,
all their little gestures, are brim full and overflowing
with hope.
Sparkling, overflowing with innocence.
Which is the very innocence of hope.

Confidence, unique innocence.

Confidence, inimitable innocence.

Ignorance of the child, innocence beside whom saintliness itself, the purity of the saint is only refuse and decay.

Confidence, ignorance, innocence of heart.

Youthfulness of heart.

Hope; the childhood of the heart.

Gentle children, inimitable children, little brothers of Jesus.

Young children.

Children beside whom the greatest saints are only age and decay.

Children that is why you are the masters and command in the homes.

We know why.

A look, a word from you and the most stubborn heads are bowed.

You are the masters and we well know it.

We well know why.

Each of you is a child Jesus.

And what man, what fool, what blasphemer would dare to call himself a man Jesus.

What saint, what very great saint, would even dare to think it.

And you too very well know that you are masters in the homes.

Your voice says so, your gaze says so, and your curls, and your mischievous expression.

And when you ask for something, you ask laughingly because you are sure of getting it.

You know very well you will get it.

On the Imitation of Jesus.   You children imitate Jesus.

Without noticing it, without knowing it, without seeing it.

And you very well know it.

And man, what man, the greatest saint, what saint does not
know that he is infinitely far from Jesus.
In his imitation.

Irreparable loss, descent, fall, inevitable waste of life.
Which is existence and life and even growing old.
To our childhood we join Jesus.
And as we grow up we are separated, we separate ourselves for
our whole life.

Children your ignorance, your confidence, your innocence is the
very ignorance and the very innocence of Jesus, of the child
Jesus.
And his timid confidence.
You are hopes as the child Jesus was a hope.
Really you are the little Jesus.

That is why, children, we are so happy that you are the masters
and that you command in the homes.
That is the very commandment of hope.
Your reign is hope's own reign.
For we men what are we.
With our poor imitation.

And your commandment is the very commandment of Jesus.

Strange fate, strange destiny, destination of man.
When we are children, we are the little Jesus, we join the
child Jesus.
And when we are men, separate what are we.

Handsome children, your gaze is the very gaze of Jesus.

Your blue gaze.
Of the child Jesus.
Your beautiful gaze.
Your brow is the very brow of Jesus.
Your voice the very voice of Jesus.

And we what are we.
With our veiled gaze.
Our veiled brow.
Our veiled voice.
And at the corners of our lips the curl of bitterness.
And at best the curl of penitence.
We are never more than innocence regained.
And they are the first innocence.

What becomes of us.
What has become of us.
What do we know.
What can we do.
What do we do.
What do we have.
We never have anything but restored innocence.
And they have the first innocence.
And supposing the best, at the very best, taking everything
    for the best we would never be anything but innocence
    conserved.
But they are the first innocence.
And as much as ripe fruit, just ripe, taken from the tree, is
    superior to conserved fruit,
Fresh is better than conserved fruit.
So the innocence of the child is superior to the innocence
    of man.
Is worth more than what man no longer even dares to call his
    innocence.

He thinks of his three children who at this very moment are
   playing by the hearth.
Are they playing, are they working, it is impossible to tell.
With children.
Are they working with their mother.
It is never possible to tell
Children are not like men.
For children, playing, working, resting, stopping, running,
   are all one.
All the same.
Are all the same thing.   They make no distinction.
They are happy.
They enjoy themselves all the time.   As much when they are
   working as when they are playing.
They do not even notice.
They are very happy.
So their commandment is the very commandment of Jesus.
Of the child Jesus.
Hope also is she who enjoys herself all the time.

He thinks of his three children who are playing at this
   moment by the hearth.
If only they are happy.
Isn't that all a father asks.
We live for them, we ask only that our children be happy.

He thinks of his children whom he placed especially under
   the protection of the Blessed Virgin.
One day when they were ill.
And when he was greatly frightened.
He still shudders when he thinks of that day.
When he was so frightened.
For them and for himself.
Because they were ill.

He had trembled in his shoes.

At the very idea that they were ill.

He had understood that he could not live like that.

With his children ill.

And his wife who was so frightened.

So terribly frightened.

That her gaze was absent, her brow wrinkled and she said not
a word.

Like an animal in pain.

That is silent.

For her heart was wrung.

She breathed like a woman being strangled.

Her heart in a vise.

Her throat in the grip of fingers; in the jaws of a vise.

His wife who was gritting her teeth, tightening her lips.

And who hardly spoke and whose voice was strange.

Whose voice belonged to someone else.

So terribly frightened she was.

And did not want to admit it.

But he, heaven knows was a man.   He was not afraid to speak.

He had understood perfectly that things could not go on like
that.

Things could not continue.

Like that.

He could not live with his children ill.

Then he had taken a step (a daring step), he still laughed when
he thought about it.

He even admired himself a little for it.   And truly he had some
reason to.   And he still shivered at the thought of it.

You have to admit that he had been awfully bold and that it was
a bold step.

And yet all Christians can do the same.

You even wonder why they do not.

Just as you pick up three children and put all three of them.

Together.   At the same time.

For fun.   As in a game.

In the arms of their mother and nurse who laughs.
And protests.
Because there are too many.
And she will not have the strength to hold them.
He, boldly like a man.
He had picked up, in prayer he had picked up.
(France must go on, Christendom must go on.)
His three children from where they were lying in illness and
    misery.
And calmly he had put them.
In prayer he had put them.
Calmly into the arms of her who bears all the sorrow of the world.
And whose arms are so full.
For the Son took all the sins.
But the Mother took all the sorrow.

He had said, in his prayer he had said: I am worn out.
I can't make it out.   It is too much for me.
I don't want to hear any more about it.
It is not my business.
(France must go on, Christendom must go on.)
Take them.   I give them to you.   Do as you wish with them.
I have had enough.
She who was the mother of Jesus Christ can very well also be
    the mother of these two little boys and this little girl.
Who are brothers of Jesus Christ.
And for whom Jesus Christ came into the world.
What difference does it make to you.   You have so many others.
What difference does it make to you, one more or less.
(He meant world without end, all the children of men, all the
    brothers of Jesus, the little brothers, and she will have
    so many others world without end.)
A man must have a nerve to speak that way.
To the Blessed Virgin.
With tears on his eyelashes, with the words on his lips, he

was speaking, in prayer he was speaking thus.

Inwardly.

He was very angry, God forgive him, he still shivers over it
(but he is awfully glad to have thought of it).

(The foolish man, as if it were he who had thought of it, the
poor man.)

He was speaking with great anger (God keep him) and with great
violence and, inwardly, within this great anger and this
great violence there was great devotion.

You see them, he was saying, I am giving them to you. And I
am going home, I am escaping so that you cannot give them
back to me.

I'll have no more to do with them. You can see that.

How he congratulated himself on having had the courage to take
that step.

Not everyone would have dared.

He was happy, he was congratulating himself laughing and trembling.

(He had not spoken of it to his wife.

He had not dared. Women may be jealous.

It is better not to create trouble in one's home.

And to have peace.

He had arranged that all alone.

It is safer and less trouble.)

Since that time everything had been going well.

Naturally.

How could things go otherwise.

Than well.

Since it was the Blessed Virgin who was taking over.

Who had taken the responsibility.

She knows better than we do.

And She, who had taken them, although she had others before
those three.

(He had taken a unique step.

Why don't all Christiams take it?)

36

He had been awfully bold.

Nothing ventured nothing gained.

Only the faint-hearted lose.

It is even strange that all Christians do not do the same.

It is so simple.

You never think of the simple thing.

We search and search, we go to great pains, we never think
    of the thing that is simplest.

Anyway we are stupid, might as well say so at once.

And She, who had taken them, although she had no lack.

She had others before those three, she would have others, she
    had others afterward.

She had had others, she would have others world without end.

And She, who had taken them, he knew all along that she would
    take them.

She would not have the heart ot leave them orphaned.

(How cowardly he had been, all the same.)

She could not leave them beside a boundary-stone.

(That is what he was counting on, the rascal.)

She was forced to take them,

She who had taken them.

He was still congratulating himself over it.

And yet we are so proud of having children.

(But men are not jealous.)

Of seeing them eat and seeing them grow up.

And in the evening of seeing them sleep like angels.

And of kissing them morning and evening, and at noon.

Right on the crown of their heads.

When they innocently bow their heads as a colt lowers his head.

As supple as a colt, as playful as a colt.

With necks as supple.

And the whole body and back.

Like the supple growing stalk of a healthy plant.

Of a young plant.

Like the very stalk of growing hope.

Laughingly they bend their backs like a young, handsome colt,
    their necks and their heads together.

In order to present to their father, to the kiss of their
    father the exact crown of their heads.

This point, right on the crown of the head, this center around
    which all the hair swirls in spirals.

They enjoy doing this.

(They are always enjoying themselves.)

They make a game of it.

They make a game of everything.

They hum, they sing songs that you never heard of and that they
    invent as they go along, they sing all the time.

And in the same movement they straighten up almost without
    pausing.

Like a young stalk swaying in the wind that returns upright
    naturally.

For them their father's kiss is a game, an amusement, a ceremony.

A welcome.

Something taken for granted, very good, unimportant.

A simple thing.

To which they do not even pay attention.

So to speak,

It is so much a habit.

So much their due.

Their hearts are pure.

They receive it as they would a piece of bread.

They play with it, they enjoy it as they would a piece of bread.

Their father's kiss.   It is their daily bread.   If they sus-
    pected what it is for their father.

The wretches.   But that is not their business.

They have plenty of time to know that later.

They only think, when their eyes meet their father's gaze.
That he seems not to enjoy himself enough.
In life.

And children when they weep.
That is infinitely better than when we laugh.
For they weep in hope.
And we laugh only in faith and in charity.

So he has put his children in a safe place and he is glad and
    he laughs to himself and even laughs aloud and rubs his
    hands together.
Over the good trick he has played.
I mean over the great discovery that he made.   The step he
    took.
(The fact is also that he could not go on.)
He gave his children calmly into the arms of the Blessed Virgin.
And off he went with his arms free.

He went off empty-handed.
He who had given them away.
Like a man who was carrying a basket.
And who was exhausted and whose shoulders ached.
And who put his basket on the ground.
Or handed it to somebody.

He is not like a man who has hired out his children on a farm.
For he who has hired out his children on a farm.
Remains the owner of his children.
And it is the farmer who becomes the hirer.   The farmer.
He on the contrary wants only to be the hirer of his children.
He has only a life interest.

And it is God who has full ownership.
But he is a good owner, is God.

Admire the wisdom of this man.
This man who now wants only to be the hirer of his children.
This man who goes off, who goes home with empty hands.
For God is not jealous, nor is the Blessed Virgin.
They will calmly leave him all the enjoyment of his children.
It is pleasant to have God as the owner.

The man is clever, he has given his children into the arms
    of the Blessed Virgin, into the hands of God.
Of God their creator.
And their owner.
Is not all creation in the hands of God.
Is not all creation the property of God.

When children weep they are happier than we are when we laugh.
And when they are sick they are more wretched than anyone.
And more touching.
Because we feel and because they feel that it is already
A curtailing of their childhood.
And the first sign of their growing old.
Of death.
Temporal death.

And she, who had taken them, was
So touching and so beautiful. (While he went off with a light

heart.)

And she, who had taken them, was
So touching and so pure.
Not only filled with faith and charity.
But even filled with hope.
Pure and young like hope. (While off he went with his arms
   free.)
And she, who had taken them, was
In her tender youth. (While off he went his hands empty.)
And she, who had taken them, was
In her eternal youth.

There are days in life when you feel that you can no longer
   be satisfied with patron saints.
No offense intended.
(And she, who had taken them, was
So burdened with family.)
You feel that patron saints no longer suffice.
(No offense intended.)
There is a great danger and you have to go higher up.
It is better to deal with God than his saints. *
(And she, who had taken them, was
So touching and so pure.
Mater Dei, mother of God,
Mother of Jesus and of all men his brothers.
The brothers of Jesus.)
You have to go straight up to God and the Blessed Virgin.
(And she, who had taken them, had
So many children in her charge.
All the children of men.
Since this first little one she had carried in her arms.
The little fellow who laughed like a jewel.
And who had since caused her so much suffering.

---

*French proverb.

41

Because he had died for the salvation of the world.)
And she, who had taken them, was
So loving and so pure.   There are days when you feel that you
    can no longer be satisfied with ordinary saints.
That ordinary saints no longer suffice.   And she, who had taken
    them, was
So young and so mighty.
So mighty with God.
So mighty with the Almighty.

And she, who had taken them, was
So burdened with sorrows.
And she had known so many since that little fellow.
Who laughed as he nursed.
It is a long time now since she was the mother of Seven
    Sorrows.
The seven sorrows were just a beginning.
For a long time she has been and we have made her
The mother of seventy and of seventy times seventy sorrows.

While he, who had handed them over, went off with his mind
    free and his eyes untroubled.
Like a man who has made a good bargain.
Carefree, his brows clear, relaxed.
His brow unwrinkled.
Like a man who has just escaped a great danger.
And truly he had just escaped the greatest danger of all.
And she, who had taken them, was
So eternally concerned.
And she had taken them under her protection and into her charge.
(After so many others, along with so many others.)
And in commendam for eternity.

And thus she who is not only

All faith and all charity.

But also all hope.

And that is seven times more difficult.

As it is also seven times more gracious.

So she took under her protection and into her charge.

And in commendam for eternity.

The young virtue Hope.

The truth must be told.   Still he is a very great saint is
   Saint Marcel.

And a very great patron.

(Although we don't know exactly what he did.

   But we mustn't say so.

And perhaps there have even been several.

But anyway he was a great saint, let's say a saint, that's
   indeed a lot.)

But there are days when one must go higher up.

We should not be afraid to speak the truth.   Still she is a
   very great saint is Saint Germaine.

And a very great patron.   Who must be very mighty.

(Although we don't know exactly what she did.

   But we mustn't say so.)

But what difference does it make, she did at least enough to
   be a saint and a great saint.   And that is indeed a lot.

It is indeed everything.

Only to be a saint is indeed everything.

And there is her fellow-sponsor Saint Germain, who may be used,
   born at Auxerre, bishop of Auxerre, who will have the eternal
   glory.

Of having consecrated to God our great saint and great patron
   and our great friend.

Saint Geneviève,
who was a simple shepherdess.

43

Saint Germain, called the Auxerrois, born at Auxerre, bishop
of Auxerre.
Bishop and saint at the time of the barbarian armies,
And the repulse of the barbarian armies,
Bishop and saint of France,
And who may be used as a patron.
As a very great patron.

And Saint Geneviève, born at Nanterre.
A Parisian, the patron saint of Paris.
Patron and saint of France, those are great patrons and great
saints.
Saint Marcel, Saint Germain, Saint Geneviève.
Still there are days when the greatest friendships do not
suffice.
Neither Marcel nor Geneviève,
Geneviève our great friend.
Neither the greatest patronage nor the greatest saintliness.
There are days when patrons and saints do not suffice.
The greatest patrons and the greatest saints.
And when we must go higher up, still higher and higher; ever
still higher.

To the utmost saintliness, the utmost purity, the utmost beauty,
the utmost patronage.

We must have the courage to speak the truth.   Saint Peter is
a great saint and a great patron among all patrons.
(We know very well what he did, but it is perhaps better not to
talk too much about it.)
But anyway he is certainly a very great patron.
For he was the cornerstone.

And the gates of Hell shall not prevail against it.

Tu es Petrus, et super hanc petram.

And eternally he is Peter and upon this rock.

And for a man who wants to go to Paradise he is indeed the
greatest patron that one can imagine.

For he is at the gate and he keeps the gate and he is the
gate-keeper and has the keys.

He is the eternal Gate-keeper and the eternal Key-bearer.

He carries at his belt the great bunch of keys.

And yet I swear that he is not a turnkey.

For he is the warder of eternal Liberty.

And in a prison, from a prison the prisoners would very much
like to escape.

But in paradise on the contrary those who are in paradise are
not on the verge of leaving.

There is no danger of their asking to leave.

You would have to pay dearly to get them to leave.

They would not want to give their places to others.

Therefore you could not find a better patron that Saint Peter.

But there comes a day, there comes an hour.

There comes a moment when Saint Marcel and Saint Germaine.

And Saint Germain himself and our great friend the great Saint
Geneviève.

And great Saint Peter himself no longer suffice.

And when you must resolutely do what must be done.

Then you must take your courage in your two hands.

And address yourself directly to her who is above all.

Be bold. Once. Address yourself boldly to her who is infinitely
beautiful.

Because she is also infinitely kind.

To her who intercedes.
The only one who can speak with the authority of a mother.

Address yourself boldly to her who is infinitely pure.
Because she is also infinitely sweet.

To her who is infinitely noble.
Because she is also infinitely gracious.
Infinitely courteous.
Courteous as the priest who goes right to the entrance of the
    church to meet the newborn baby.
On the baptismal day.
In order to usher him into the house of God..

To her who is infinitely rich.
Because she is also infinitely poor.

To her who is infinitely high.
Because she is also infinitely condescending.

To her who is infinitely great.
Because she is also infinitely small.
Infinitely humble.
A young mother.

To her who is infinitely young.
Because she is also infinitely mother.

To her who is infinitely upright.
Because she is also infinitely stooping.

To her who is infinitely joyful
Because she is also infinitely sorrowful.

Seventy and seven times seventy times sorrowful.

To her who is infinitely touching
Because she is infinitely touched.

To her who is all Greatness and all Faith.
Because she is also all Charity.

To her who is all Faith and all Charity.
Because she is also all HOPE.

Fortunately saints are not jealous of each other.
That would be the last straw.
That would be a bit too much.
And fortunately they are not jealous of the Blessed Virgin.
This is actually what we call the communion of saints.
They very well know what she is like and that as much as the
    child surpasses the man in purity.
So much and seventy times so much she surpasses them in purity.

As much as the child surpasses the man in youth.
So much and seventy times so much she surpasses the saints
    (even the greatest saints), in youth and in childhood.

As much as the child surpasses the man in hope.
So much and seventy times so much she surpasses the saints
    (even the greatest saints), in faith, charity and HOPE.

Man cannot compare with a child in purity, youth, and hope.
In childhood.
In innocence.
In ignorance.
In weakness.
In newness.
Thus, so much and seventy times so much the saints, the
    greatest saints.

Do not compare with her in childhood and in purity.
In innocence and youth.
In ignorance, in weakness, in newness.
In faith, in charity, in hope.

Geneviève, my child, was a simple shepherdess.
Jesus too was a simple shepherd.
But what a shepherd my child.
Shepherd of what a flock.   Pastor of what sheep.
In what a country of the world.
Pastor of the hundred sheep that remained in the fold, pastor
    of the sheep that went astray, pastor of the sheep that
    returns.
And who to help it return, for its legs can no longer bear it
    up,
Its worn-out legs,
Picks it up gently and carries it back himself on his shoulders.
On his two shoulders.
Gently wrapped in a half circle around the back of his neck,
The head of the sheep gently resting thus on his right shoulder.
Which is the good side.
On the right shoulder of Jesus,
Which is the side of the good souls,
And its body half bent around his neck.
Around his neck in a half wreath,
Like a wool scarf that keeps you warm.
So the sheep even keeps its own pastor warm,
The woolly sheep.
Its two forefeet well and properly held in his right hand,
Which is the good side,
Held tight,
Gently but firmly.
The two hind feet well and properly held in his left hand,
Gently but firmly.
As you hold a child when you play at carrying it astride

Your shoulders,

His right leg in your right hand, his left leg in your left
   hand.

Just so the Savior, just so the good pastor, which means the
   good shepherd

Carries back on his shoulders this sheep that had gone astray,
   that was going to be lost

So that the stones of the road should no longer wound its
   wounded feet.

Because there will be more joy in heaven over the sinner who
   returns.

Than for the hundred righteous that did not leave the fold.

For the hundred righteous who did not leave the fold.

Must have remained only in faith and charity.

But the sinner who strayed and was almost lost

By his very departure and because he was going to be absent
   from the evening roll-call

Caused the birth of fear and thus the welling up of hope
   itself

In the very heart of God,

In the heart of Jesus

The trembling of fear and its chill,

The tremor of hope.

Through this strayed sheep Jesus knew fear in love.

And the trembling that divine hope puts in charity itself.

And God was afraid of having to doom it.

Through this sheep and because it was not returning to the
   fold and was going to be absent at the evening roll-call,

Jesus like a man knew human anxiety,

Jesus made man,

Knew what anxiety is at the very heart of charity.
Anxiety gnawing at the heart of charity thus worm-eaten,
But thus also he knew the very first sign of the sprouting of
    hope.
When the young virtue hope begins to sprout in the heart of man,
Under his rough husk,
Like the first budlet of April.

So Geneviève was a shepherdess but Mary
Is the mother of the shepherd himself
And as long as there is a fold,
That is a sheep-fold,
She will be the mother of the eternal shepherd.

Then one day you must go right up
To her who intercedes.
Beyond Marcel and Germaine and Germain,
Geneviève and Saint Peter.
Beyond the patrons, the saints,
Beyond the eternal patron of Paris.
And even beyond the eternal patron of Rome
You must go up
To her who is the most awe-inspiring.
Because she is also the most maternal.

To her who is infinitely white.
Because she is also the mother of the Good Shepherd,
of the Man who hoped.

(And he was quite right to hope, since he succeeded in bringing
    back the sheep.)
To her who is infinitely celestial.

Because she is also infinitely terrestrial.

To her who is infinitely eternal
Because she is also infinitely temporal.

To her who is infinitely above us.
Because she is also infinitely among us.

To her who is the mother and queen of angels.
Because she is also the mother and queen of men.
Queen of heaven, regent of earth.

(Empress of the infernal marshes.)

To her who is Mary.
Because she is full of grace.

To her who is full of grace
Because she is with us.

To her who is with us.
Because the Lord is with her.
To her who intercedes.
Because she is blessed among women.
And because Jesus, the fruit of her womb, is blessed.

To her who is full of grace.
Because she is full of grace.

To her who is infinitely queen
Because she is the humblest of creatures.
Because she was a poor woman, a wretched woman, a poor Jewess

of Judea.

To her who is infinitely remote
Because she is infinitely near.

To her who is the most exalted princess
Because she is the humblest of women.

To her who is closest to God
Because she is closest to men.

To her who is infinitely safe
Because in her turn she saves infinitely.
To her who is most pleasing to God.

To her who is full of grace
Because she is also full of efficacity
Now

And because she is full of grace and efficacity
And at the hour of our death amen.

For having conceived and for having given birth,
For having nourished and having borne
The Man who feared,
The Man who hoped.

And he was quite right to hope, since he succeeded in saving
   so many saints.   At least in the beginning.   Anyway in short
   he succeeded all the same.

To her who is the only Queen

Because she is the humblest of subjects.

To her own is first after God
Because she is first before man.

First before men and women.
First before sinners.

First before saints.
First before carnal man.

And also indeed first before the very angels.

Listen, my child, I am going to explain to you, listen to me
    carefully,
I am going to explain to you why,
how, and wherefore
the holy Virgin is a creature unique, rare,
Of infinite rarity,
Excelling all others,
Unique among all creatures.
Follow me closely.   I do not know whether you will understand
    me clearly.
All creation was pure.   Follow me closely.
(In short Jesus succeeded, we must not be too difficult.
We must not be too demanding.
Of life.
Since all the same he was able to bring back, to gather the
    sheaf of saints.
That ascending he cast at the feet of his father.
And the souls of the righteous that he had perfumed with his
    virtues.)
So all creation was pure.
As it had come, as it had sprung pure and young and new from
    the hands of its Creator.

But the sin of Satan attracted, corrupted half of the angels.
And the sin of Adam attracted, corrupted all men in their
   blood.

So that nothing pure remained but half the angels
And nothing among men,
Nobody among men,
In all creation,
Of the original purity, the young purity, the first purity,
   the created purity, the childlike purity, the purity of
   creation itself.

When there was created this unique nature,
Blessed among women,

Infinitely unique, infinitely rare,
Now.

Infinitely pleasing to God.
And at the hour of our death amen,
Excelling all others.

When finally, when one day in time there was created for eternity,
For the salvation of the world this unique being.
To be the Mother of God.
To be woman and yet to be pure.

Listen carefully, my child, follow me closely, it is difficult
   to explain.
In what way she is such a unique being.   But follow me closely.
Something is lacking in every being.
Not only they are not the Creator,

54

God their creator.
(This is natural.
Perfectly natural.)
That they are not their own Creator.
But in addition there is always something lacking.
What those who are carnal lack is precisely purity.
We know that.
What those who are pure lack is precisely carnality.
You must know that.

But she on the contrary lacks nothing.
Unless truly being God himself.
Being her own Creator.
(But this is natural.)

For although carnal she is pure.
And although pure, she is carnal.

And it is for this reason that she is not only a woman unique
    among women.
But she is a being unique among beings.

Literally first after God.   After the Creator.
Immediately after.
The one whom you find immediately below God
In the celestial hierarchy.

After this disaster.   After this fault.   After this failure.
After this disaster of half the angels and all the men, nothing
    carnal remained that was pure,
Of the purity of birth.

When one day this woman was born of the tribe of Juda
For the salvation of the world
Because she was full of grace.

And besides Joseph was of the house of David
Which was the house of Jacob.
When she was born filled with the first innocence.
As pure as Eve before the first sin.

See that you do not despise one of these little ones: for I
    tell you, their angels in heaven always behold the face of
    my Father in heaven.
For the Son of man came to save what was lost.
What do you think? If a man have a hundred sheep, and one of
    them stray,
(Takes the wrong road);
will he not leave the ninety-nine in the mountains, and go in
    search of the one that has strayed?
And if he happen to find it, verily I say to you, he rejoices
    over it more than over the ninety-nine that did not go astray.
Even so it is not the will of your Father in heaven that a
    single one of these little ones should perish.

The Good Pastor in other words the good shepherd.
Through it he knew anxiety.
Through the one that did not remain with the ninety-nine others.
Deadly anxiety.
(Devouring anxiety in the heart of Jesus.)
The anxiety of not finding it again. Of not knowing.
Of never finding it again. Human anxiety.
The deadly anxiety of having to doom it.
But finally he is saved.
The savior himself is saved.

He is saved from having to doom it.
How freely he breathes.
Anyway there is one saved.
He will not have to doom that soul.

Through this little sheep that had only taken the wrong road,
(Which can happen to anyone,)

et erraverit una ex eis,
and it has happened to the greatest saints
To take the road of sin
Through this little sheep of a soul man, made man, he knew
    man's anxiety.
But through this foolish little sheep of a soul (that frightened
    him so much) man, made man, he knew man's hope.

Through this little worthless sheep that had gone astray,
    through this sheep creature
Man, made man, he knew budding hope,
The budding of hope which springs up in the heart sweeter
    than a delicate budlet of April.

In all beings something is lacking, besides not being the
    Creator.
Those who are carnal, we know, lack purity.
But those who are pure, you must know, lack carnality.
A single being is both carnal and pure.
It is for this reason that the Blessed Virgin is not only the
    greatest blessing that has befallen earth.
But even the greatest blessing that has been granted in all
    creation.
She is not only first among women.

Blessed among women,

She is not only first among all beings,

She is a unique being, infinitely unique, infinitely rare.

A single one and no other both carnal and pure.

    Since as for the angels

They would indeed be pure, but they are pure spirits, they are
    not carnal.

They do not know what it is to have a body, to be a body.

They do not know what it is to be this poor

Carnal creature.

A body moulded of the clay of this earth.

This carnal earth.

They do not know this mysterious bond, this created bonding,

Infinitely mysterious,

Of the soul and body.

For God did not create only the soul and the body.

The immortal soul and the mortal body which will be restored
    to life.

But he also created, in a terse act of creation he created

This mysterious link, this created linking,

This welding, this bonding of body and soul,

Of spirit and matter,

Of the immortal and the mortal which will be restored to life

And the soul is linked to mud and dust.

To mud when it rains and to dust in dry weather.

And yet, linked thus, the soul must work out its salvation.

Like a good plough-horse, like a strong and faithful animal,
    like a great Lorrainese work-horse that pulls the plow.

By his vigor and strength he must not only move himself, pull
    himself, drag himself.

Stand on his four feet.

But by this same vigor and strength he must also move and pull
    and drag the inert plow.

Inert otherwise, that cannot move by itself, pull or drag
  itself all alone,
Move, drag, pull, otherwise.
Inert otherwise, but hard-working with the horse, industrious
  and active with his help.
This plow behind that tills the land of Lorraine.
(But that plows only on condition that it is pulled.)
As the plow-horse, good beast, must not only carry and move
  himself,
On his four legs, on his four feet,
But also drag the plow which, thus brought to life, tills the
  earth behind,
So the soul, that plough-horse, whose tilling is terrestrial,
Whose tilling is carnal,
Must not only move and carry itself on the four virtues,
Pull and drag itself.
But it must move and carry,
It must also pull and drag
The body sunken in earth that plows behind the soil of earth.
This inert body, otherwise lifeless,
Which animated by the soul can industriously plow the earth,
Succeed in plowing it.
The soul must not only work out its salvation, for its own sake,
It must also work out the salvation of the body, the soul's
  salvation for the sake of the body.
And it must at the same time find salvation for the body which
  will be restored to life.
Their common salvation, their double salvation so that after
  the last judgment,
Immediately afterward,
Together they may share in eternal joy,
The immortal soul and the mortal body dead but restored to
  life,
Having become a body in glory.
As two hands are joined in prayer,
And one is no more upright than the other,

So the body and the soul are like two joined hands.
And both together will enter eternal life.
And they will be two joined hands, together, for what is
    infinitely more than prayer.
And infinitely more than the sacrament.
Or both together they will fall like two wrists bound together
Into eternal captivity.

As a good ploughman in order to plow this heavy soil,
Which sticks to the ploughshare,
Harnesses a strong horse to the plow (itself strong,
But by itself inert),
(And he does not put the plow before the oxen,)
Just so the Lord God in order to till this carnal soil,
This heavy soil that sticks to the body and heart of man,
This heavy soil,
This terrestrial
And earthy soil,

(Queen of heaven, regent of earth,)

So the Lord God has harnessed the soul to the body.

And as the plow-horse must pull for himself and for the plow,
Just so the soul must pull for itself and for the body,
Must work out its salvation, their salvation, its own and the
    body's.
For neither of the two will be saved without the other.
We have no choice. We must be two hands joined or two wrists
    bound together.
Two hands joined that rise joined to bliss.
Two wrists bound that fall down bound into captivity.
The hands will not be disjoined nor the wrists unbound.
For God himself has bonded the immortal to the mortal.

And to the dead man who will be restored to life.

That is something, my child, that angels do not know.
I mean that is something they have not experienced.
What it is to have this body; to have this bond with the body;
    to be this body.
To have this bond with the earth, with this earth, to be this
    earth, the slime and dust, the ashes and mud of the earth,
<u>The very body of Jesus.</u>

So the soul must work not only for itself.
But it must work also for its servant the body.
As a rich man who wants perchance to cross a bridge
Pays the toll-collector who has a little shelter at the
    entrance to the bridge.
Pays a penny for himself and a penny also for the servant who
    follows him.
Just so the soul must pay for the soul and the body, the soul
    must work for the soul and the body.
For it is always the soul that is a rich man,
And no matter what the poor body does, or says, with all its
    pride it will never be anything but a poor creature
And always in the wrong.
(Even when it is right.)
Especially when it is right.

That is something, my child, that the angels do not know, I
    mean that they have not experienced.

The sins of the flesh and the unique remissions of the flesh.

Sins which are of the flesh and are only of the flesh.

And of which every being who is not carnal is unaware.
Sins of the flesh and of the terrestrial earth that angels
 know only by hearsay.
Like a story from another world.
And almost so to speak from another creation.

Carnal sins that the angels do not know.
I mean that they have not experienced.

Sins of the body and of the terrestrial heart.
(Redeemed by the body and the heart.)
Sins of the flesh and the blood.
(Redeemed by the flesh and the Blood.)

Terrestrial sins.
Earth-bound sins.
Earthy sins.
Sins of the soil.
And of the terrestrial earth.

The first carnal sin, when suddenly your blood rises and beats
 in your temples, in a fit of anger.
In a burst of anger.
The sin of anger.

The second carnal sin, my child, the greatest sin that ever
 befell the world.
When the blood grows faint in the heart, the sin of despair.

And on the road of despair, my child, the greatest temptation
 that ever offered itself in the world.
When the blood trembles and beats wildly in the heart.
The greatest carnal temptation
But is it really a temptation.

The temptation to mortal anxiety.

When the Shepherd himself was afraid and trembled in his heart.

Lest he have to doom it, to lose it, I mean to let it be lost.

The mortal fear, the mortal anxiety of having to condemn to
    death.

I mean more exactly of having to let it be condemned to death.

In montibus, in the mountains, when he was afraid of never
    finding it again.

Of being forced

To leave it lost in the night

Of eternal death.

The sins of the flesh, but the remissions of the flesh,

They do not know the carnal remissions either.

This infinite, eternal and sudden remission.

Inseparably both temporal and carnal.

When all the sins of the world together suddenly.

Were redeemed by the crucifixion of a man's body.

When the thorns of the crown of thorns caused drops of a man's
    blood to drip from his brow.

When the four nails in his limbs caused a man's blood to drip
    on the ground and on the wood of the cross.

When the Roman lance, piercing a man's side, caused a man's
    blood to run down his flank.

And preceding this remission

This total this global remission

As the eldest prince in the procession of the king precedes
    the golden orb of sovereignty,

And as a child in a procession precedes the Body itself and
    the Holy Sacrament,

Preceding all remission they do not know what is almost sweeter
    than the remission itself.

So to speak.

When the blood stirs and begins to flow slowly toward the heart,

Young hope,
The welling of hope,
When young blood begins to flow back toward the heart.
As the young sap of April begins to rise, to run beneath the
hard bark.

What a commandment, what authority, what brutality, what a
crushing of hope.
See that you do not despise one of these little ones:
Not one:
for I tell you,
their angels in heaven
always behold the face of my Father in heaven,
As you see, as you feel the sap in the month of May
Rise beneath the hard bark,
Just so you feel, just so you see in the month of Easter
New blood stir and rise
Under the hard husk of the heart,
Under the husk of anger, under the husk of despair,
Under the hard husk of sin.

There is something that they do not know, nor the greatest
carnal sin.
When the blood rises and swells and tumefies in the heart and
head.
When in a sudden burst, in a huge burst the blood rises and
swells and boils.
In a fit of pride.
When the blood, like a beast, leaps, suddenly,
Like a bird of prey, like a breast of prey
In a fit of pride.
Pride, the greatest sin that ever befell the earth
And all creation.
Pride of body, pride of blood, pride of the flesh.
That swells and buzzes in the whole body like a tempest of
buzzing.

And that beats in the temples like a roll on the drum.
Ancient pride, old as the race, old as the flesh,
And like the sap of the birch.
Like the sap and the blood of pride, like the sap and the
    blood of the oak
Carnal pride that is what they do not know,
What they have never experienced at all.
They had their pride also, I mean those who were lost
On account of pride, Lucifer, Satan.   Their pride of perdition.
But it was a pale pride, a bloodless pride,
A pride of the mind, of the head,
Not at all a pride of heart and blood,
Not at all a pride of body,
Not at all a pride of this terrestrial
Earth.

It was a pride of thought, a poor pride of ideas.
A pale pride, a vain pride all in their heads.
Smoke.
Not at all a great stout pride nourished on fat and blood.
Bursting with health.
Skin shining.
Which also could only be redeemed by flesh and blood.

A pride puffed up with blood
Which buzzes in the ears
With the buzzing of blood,
A pride that makes your eyes bloodshot,
And drums in your temples,
That is something that they do not know.

So they do not know that Easter exists
Easter day, Easter Sunday
Easter week

Easter month.
For the rising, for the renewal of carnal hope
As for the sap of the oak and the birch
There exists a month of April, a month of May.

They do not know all this carnal pride, this full carnal pride,
    this hot carnal pride,
Of boiling blood.
So they do not know the carnal remission
Of the blood that was shed.

They do not know the great pride of man,
Full of itself.
Fat.
Swollen, nourished on itself.
They do not know so much fatness so much sustenance
Which could only be atoned for
By the frightening, by the frightful emaciation,
By the skeletal thinness
Of Jesus on the cross.

They do not know the old royal pride, they do not know the
    ancient pride,
The full-blooded pride, bursting with self, the pride that
    bursts with conceit, so they do not know
That young, timid hope
Walks at the head of the procession,
Advances innocently
Because she is heir apparent of France.

What brutality, my child, what an imposition, what violence
    of God.
What a defeat, what a commandment of hope.
<u>See that you do not despise</u> A SINGLE <u>one of these little ones:</u>
<u>For I tell you,</u>
<u>Their angels in heaven always behold the face of my Father,</u>
<u>In heaven.</u>
Jesus Christ, my child, did not come to tell us idle tales.
You understand, he did not make the trip to earth,
A long trip between you and me,
(And he was so comfortable where he was.)
(Before coming.
He did not have all our cares.)
He did not make the trip down to earth
To come and tell us diverting stories
And jokes.
There is no time for amusement.
He did not use, he did not employ, he did not spend
The thirty-three years of his earthly life,
Of his carnal life.
The thirty years of his private life,
The three years of his public life,
The three days of his passion and death,
(And in limbo the three days of his sepulchre,)
He did not use, he did not employ, he did not spend all that,
His thirty years of work and his three years of preaching and
    his three days of passion and death,
His thirty-three years of prayer,
His incarnation, which is properly his assumption of flesh,
His assumption of carnality, of humanity and his crucifixion
    and entombment,
His embodiment in flesh and his agony,
His life as a man and his life as a workman and his life as a
    priest and his life as a saint and his life as a martyr,
His life of faith,

His life of Jesus,
In order to come then (at the same time) to spin yarns for us.
He did not use, he did not employ he did not spend all that.
He did not assume all this expense
This great expense
In order to come to give us, then
Riddles
To guess
Like a magician.
Acting clever.
No, my child, and neither did Jesus give us dead words
That we are to shut up in little boxes
(Or in big ones,)
And that we are to preserve in rancid oil
Like Egyptian mummies.
Jesus Christ, my child, did not give us preserved words
To keep,
But he gave us living words
To nourish.
Ego sum via, veritas et vita,
I am the way, the truth and the life.
Words of life, living words can only be preserved alive,
Nourished alive,
Nourished, borne, warmed, warm in a living heart.
Not preserved mustily in little wooden or cardboard boxes.
As Jesus put on, was forced to put on the body, to be clothed
    in flesh
In order to pronounce these (carnal) words and in order to
    make them heard,
In order to be able to pronounce them,
So we, just so we, in imitation of Jesus,
So we, who are flesh, we must profit from it,
Profit from our carnal state in order to preserve them, to
    warm them, to nourish them living and carnal in ourselves,
(That is something even the angels do not know, my child,

something they have not experienced.)
As a carnal mother nourishes and warms her last born on her
    heart,
Her carnal nursling, on her breast,
Carefully held in the fold of her arm,
So, profiting from our carnal state,
We must nourish, we have to nourish in our hearts,
With our flesh and our blood,
With our hearts,
The carnal Words,
The eternal Words, temporally carnally pronounced.
Miracle of miracles, my child, mystery of mysteries.
Because Jesus Christ became our carnal brother
Because he pronounced temporally and carnally the eternal words,
In monte, on the mountain,
It is to us, weak as we are, that it has been given,
It is on us, weak and carnal as we are, that it depends,
To make alive and to nourish and to keep alive in time
These living words pronounced in time.
Mystery of mysteries, this privilege has been given to us,
This unbelievable, exorbitant privilege,
Of keeping alive the words of life,
Of nourishing with our blood, with our flesh, with our hearts
Words which if it were not for us would lose their substance.

To assure (it is unbelievable), to assure for the eternal words
In addition as it were a second eternity,
A temporal and carnal eternity, an eternity of flesh and blood,
Nourishment, an eternity of the body,
An earthly eternity.

Therefore the words of Jesus, the eternal words are the nurslings,
    the living nurslings of our blood and of our hearts

Of us who live in time.

Like the meanest peasant woman, if the queen in her palace
  cannot nourish the prince

Because she has not enough milk,

Then the meanest peasant woman of the meanest parish can be
  summoned to the palace,

Provided she is a good nurse,

She can be summoned to nourish a son of France,

Just so all we children of all the parishes

Are summoned to nourish the word of the son of God.

O misery, O misfortune, it is our duty,

It is our task, it is our responsibility

To see that it is heard world without end,

To make it resound.

O misery, O happiness, it is our responsibility,

Tremor of happiness,

We who are nothing, we who spend on earth a few worthless
  years,

A few poor wretched years,

(We immortal souls,)

O danger, peril of death, it is we who are given the task,

We who are helpless, who are nothing, who are not assured of
  tomorrow,

Nor of to-day, who are born and die like ephemeral creatures,

Who move on like hirelings,

Still it is we who are given the task,

We who in the morning are not sure of the evening,

Nor even of noon,

And who in the evening are not sure of the morrow,

Of tomorrow morning,

It is madness, still it is we who are given the task it is our
  responsibility

To assure a second eternity to the Words,

A second eternal eternity.

A strange perpetuity.

It is our task, it is our responsibility to assure for the
    words

Eternal perpetuity, carnal perpetuity,

A perpetuity nourished with meat, fat and blood.

We who are nothing, who do not endure,

Who hardly endure at all

(On earth)

It is madness, still it is we who have the task of preserving
    and nourishing

On earth

The eternal words that were spoken, the word of God.

Mystery, danger, happiness, misfortune, grace of God, unique
    choice,

frightening responsibility, misery, splendor of our life,

we ephemeral beings, that is to say we who spend only a day.

who endure only a day,

poor migratory women who work like hirelings,

who stop in a district only to harvest the wheat or to gather
    the grapes,

who hire ourselves out for wages for two or three weeks only,

and who immediately afterward take to the road again,

on the highway,

and turn at the corner of the poplars,

we simple travellers, poor travellers, frail travellers,

uncertain travellers,

eternal vagrants,

who enter life and immediately leave it,

as vagrants enter a farm for only one meal,

for a chunk of bread and a glass of wine,

we, weak, frail, uncertain, unworthy, feeble,

71

we shepherdesses, frivolous, fleeting, transitory,
(but no, not strangers,)
unique grace, (at the risk of what misfortune?)
It depends on us frail as we are whether the eternal word
Shall resound or shall not resound.

In carnal hearts, there, my child, is something the angels do
    not know,
Otherwise than by hearsay,
And have not themselves experienced,
In carnal hearts, in uncertain hearts, in transitory hearts,
In hearts that break
A word is preserved, is nourished
That will not be broken in all eternity.

In our frail hearts a word that will last forever.

It is for that reason, my child, for that very reason,
(You are not confused, you are getting your bearings,)
It is for this reason that France that Christendom must
    continue:
In order that the eternal word may not fall into deadly silence,
Into a carnal void.

Then it is for this very reason,
We are harking back to it, my child, you recognize the route,)
It is precisely for this reason,
It is for this very reason, it is exactly for this reason,
That none of all that,
And even nothing at all,
Absolutely nothing at all
Holds together without hope
Without young Hope,

Through her who always begins again and always promises,
Who guarantees everything.
Who guarantees tomorrow to to-day and noon and evening to the
    morning,
And life to life and even eternity to time.

Through her who guarantees, through her who promises to the
    morning the day
    In its entirety,
To the spring the year
    In its entirety,
To childhood life
    In its entirety,
To time eternity
    In its entirety,
To creation God himself
    In his entirety,
To the harvest wheat
    In his entirety.
To the vines wine
    In its entirety.
To the kingdom the king and to the king the kingdom; and thus
    all the world, both eternal and temporal, both spiritual
    and carnal
And creation and God
She holds (easily) in her little hands.
In order to assure this carnal perpetuity God must
(Miracle, it is the vessel that is broken,
That is even perpetually broken,
And loses not a drop of the liquor,)
In order that the word may not fall inert
Like a dead bird God must
Create one after another these perishable beings,
These men and women,
(Who will become sinners and saints,)

One after another the parishes and in the parishes
(Miracle of miracles the imperishable is saved from perishing
    only by the perishable)
And the eternal is maintained, is eternally nourished only
    by the temporal
And in the parishes once founded, once created,
(Lorraine, Toul, Vaucouleurs, Domrémy must go on),
In the parishes one after another these perishable beings,
One after another these perishable (immortal) souls,
And these perishable bodies and hearts
In order to nourish the living imperishable word.

God must create them, God must create some, one after another.
    Some must be born.
That's his business, that is his work, we are sure it is well
    done.
He attends to it, he will attend to it eternally.
But what is our business, alas, and our work,
On us creatures created perishable,
Once created, once born, once baptized,
Once women and Christians,
What unfortunately depends on us, fortunately,
On us one after another is the nourishing of the living word,
Is the nourishing for a space of the eternal word.
After so many others, before so many others.
Since it was spoken.
Until the gate of Judgment.

In saecula saeculorum.
World without end.
From generation to generation
Since the beginning of time.
Until the end of time
On earth.

As at the door of the church on Sundays and feast days,
When we go to mass,
Or to a burial,
We pass the holy water from hand to hand,
Step by step, one after another,
Directly from hand to hand or a sprig of consecrated box
    dipped in holy water.
To make the sign of the cross either on our living selves,
    or on the bier of one who is dead,
So that the same sign of the cross is as it were borne step
    by step by the same water,
By the agency, by the ministry of the same water,
One after another on the same breasts and the same hearts,
And on the same brows,
And even on the biers of the same dead bodies,
Just so from hand to hand, from fingers to fingers,
From finger-tip to finger-tip the eternal generations,
Which are eternally going to mass,
In the same breasts, in the same hearts until the burial of
    the world,
Relaying each other,
With the same hope pass each other the word of God.

By the agency, by the ministry of the same hope.

Through her who guarantees, through her who promises, through
    her who embodies beforehand.
Through her who promises to eternity
    Time.
To the spirit
    Flesh.
To Jesus
    A church.
To God even
    Creation, (his creation, the creation,)

Reversal, strange reversal, mad reversal,
Through her who promises to the eternal
    A temporal.
To the spiritual
    A carnal.
To the Nourishment
    A nourishment.
To the Life
    A life.
A reversal such as if
she were promising
childhood to life,
spring to the year,
morning to the day.

As the faithful pass the holy water from hand to hand,
Just so we the faithful must pass each other the word of God
    from heart to heart.
From hand to hand, from heart to heart we must pass each other
    the divine
Hope.

It is not enough that we have been created, that we have been
    born, that we have remained faithful.
It is necessary, it depends on us faithful women,
It depends on us Christian women
To assure that the eternal shall not lack the temporal,
(Strange reversal,)
That the spiritual shall not lack the carnal,
It must all be said, it is unbelievable: that eternity shall
    not lack time,
Some time, a certain time.
That the spirit shall not lack flesh.
That the soul so to speak shall not lack a body.
That Jesus shall not lack a Church,

His Church.

Nothing must be omitted: That God shall not lack his creation.

In other words it depends on us
That hope shall not deceive the world.

In other words, it must be said, it depends on us
That the greater shall not lack the lesser,
That the infinitely greater shall not lack the infinitely lesser.
That the infinitely all shall not lack the infinitely nothing.

It depends on us that the infinite shall not lack the finite.
That the perfect shall not lack the imperfect.

It is a wager, we are needed, it depends on us
That the great shall not lack the small,
That the whole shall not lack a part,
That the infinitely great shall not lack the infinitely small.
That the eternal shall not lack the perishable.

We are needed, (it is ridiculous,) we are needed in order that
    the Creator
Shall not lack his creation.

And as on the last day there will be a great sign of the cross
    on the bier of the world.
Because it will be the last burial.
So on the last day there will be a great sign of the cross of
    benediction.
Because it will be the fulfilment,

The crowning of hope.

Unique grace, a feeble being bears God.
And God can need this being.
Who can be missed in his count and his census,
When he counts his sheep, missed by his love missed by him,
Who can belie his hope.

For there is the crown of thorns but there is
The crown of hope

Which is the crown of branches of a thornless tree.

Jesus Christ, my child, did not come to tell us idle tales,
In the little time he had.
What are three years in the life of a world.
In the eternity of this world.
He had no time to waste, he did not waste his time telling us
    idle tales and giving us charades to guess.
Very witty charades.
Very ingenious charades.
A magician's riddles.
With puns and wretched wily subleties.
No, he did not waste his time and effort,
He did not have time.
His efforts, his great, his very great effort.
He did not waste, he did not expend all that, his whole being,
    everything.
He did not spend everything, he did not incur this enormous
    this terrible expenditure
Of himself, of his being, of everything,
To come after that, at that price,

To come at that price to give us the trouble

Of deciphering.

Tricks, silly nonsense, illusions, witty trickery like a village
   fortune-teller.

Like a country wag.

Like a travelling showman, a charlatan in his cart.

Like a slick city fellow, like the smartest chap in the tavern.

But when the Son of God, my child, moved from heaven and from
   the right hand of his Father.

When he moved from his seat on the right hand.

He did not incur, he did not undertake this great expenditure

He did not undertake this great inconvenience to come to tell
   us nonsense

Worthless nonsense.

Idle words.

And incomprehensible cajoleries,

But, at that price, he came to tell us what he had to tell us.

Did he not.

Quietly.

Simply, honestly.

Directly.   Primarily.

Ordinarily.

As a good man speaks to a good man,

Man to man.

He did not amuse himself obscuring all that.

He had something to tell us, he told us what he had to tell us.

He did not tell us something else.

He did not tell us other than what he had to tell us.

As he had something to say, he spoke.

It is fools who try to be smart.

And who look for difficulties where none exist.

Now when your mother sends you on an errand to the baker's,

When you go to the baker's,

You do not begin all at once to tell the baker extraordinary
   things.
You do your errand and then you come back.
You take your bread, you pay and you leave.
It is the same way with him, he came to us on an errand.
He brought us a message from his Father.
He brought us his message and he went back.
He came, he paid, (what a price!), and he goes away.
He did not begin to tell us extraordinary things.
Nothing is simpler than the word of God.
He told us only about quite ordinary things.
Very ordinary.
About the incarnation, salvation, redemption, the word of God.
Three or four mysteries.
Prayer, the seven sacraments.
Nothing is simpler than the greatness of God.
He spoke to us plainly and simply.
Without affectation or confusion.
He spoke plainly, like a simple man, bluntly, like a man of
   the town,
A man of the village.
Like a man in the street who does not choose his words and
   give himself airs.
When talking.
So, whether he spoke to us and spoke to us directly,
Or whether he spoke to us in parables,
Which are called similitudes from the Latin similitudines,*
Since he had not come to tell us idle tales,
Since he always spoke to us directly and fully
Literally,
In a down-to-earth way,
So always in response we too must listen to him and understand
   him literally.

---

*   Literally: Which we call in Latin similitudes

Directly and fully in a down-to-earth way.
Our brother, our older Brother did not delude us for the
    pleasure of being clever.
We must not wrong him for the pleasure of trying to be
    smart.
And we are wronging him if we seek tricks where there are none.
If we hear, if we seek, it we infer; if we imagine;
If we strive;
If we understand his word otherwise than as he said it.
If we even listen otherwise than as he spoke.

It is even the gravest wrong that we can do him.

If we receive him otherwise than as he gave himself.

It is the gravest insult, perhaps the only insult that we can
    cast on him.
Once a crown was made: it was a crown of thorns.
And the brow and the head bled under this mock crown.
And the blood dripped drop by drop, and the blood matted his
    hair.

But a crown has also been made, a mysterious crown.
A crown, an eternal coronation.
Entirely made, my child, entirely made of pliable thornless
    boughs.
Of budding boughs, of late March boughs.
Of April boughs and May boughs.
Of flexible boughs that are easily woven into a crown.
Without a thorn.
Docile boughs that behave well in one's fingers,
A crown has been made of budlets and buds.
Of budlets of flowers like a beautiful apple tree, of budlets
    of leaves, of budlets of boughs.
Of budlets of branches.
Of buds of flowers for flowers and fruit.

All burgeoning, all budding a crown has been made
A mysterious crown.
Eternal, in advance, swollen with sap.
Perfumed, cool on the temples, tender and fragrant.
Made for to-day, for the future, for tomorrow.
For everlasting, for the day after tomorrow.
Made of tiny tips, tender tips, of the beginnings of tips.
Leafy and flowery in advance,
Which are the tips of tender, fresh budlets.
And which have the perfume and the taste of the leaf and the
    flowers.
The taste of growth, the taste of earth.
The taste of the tree.
And in advance the taste of the fruit
Of autumn
To calm the poor brow throbbing with fever, heavy with fever,
In order to make up for, in order to compensate for the mock
    coronation,
To relieve, to soothe, to calm, to refresh the throbbing
    temples,
The feverish temples.
The burning brow, the feverish brow,
Heavy with fever, the hot temples, the migraine and the insult,
    and the headache and to allay the mockery itself.
In order to soothe, to perfume, to staunch the blood that
    matted his hair
A crown also has been made, a crown of sap, an everlasting
    crown,
And it is the crown, the crowning of hope.

As a mother makes a diadem by joining the fingertips of her
    two cool hands and placing them
Around the burning brow of her child
To soothe this burning brow, this fever,
Just so an everlasting crown has been woven to soothe the

82

burning brow.

And it was a crown of greenery.

A leafy crown.

We must have confidence in God my child.

We must hope in God.

We must trust God.

We must put our trust in God.

We must have that confidence in God that is hoping in him.

We must have that trust in God that is hoping in him.

We must have hope in God.

We must hope in God, we must have faith in God, that is all
    the same thing.

We must have that faith in God that is hoping in him.

We must believe in him, which is hoping.

We must have confidence in God, he has certainly had confidence
    in us.

We must trust God, he has certainly trusted us.

We must hope in God, he has certainly pinned his hope on us.

We must put our trust in God, he has certainly put his trust in us.

What trust.

Complete trust.

We must have faith in God, he has certainly had faith in us.

Strange mystery, the most mysterious,

God has forestalled us.

Or rather it is not a proper mystery, it is not a special
    mystery, it is a mystery that has a bearing on the mysteries.

It is a redoubling, an enlargement to infinity of all the
    mysteries.

It is a miracle. A perpetual miracle, an advance miracle,
    God forestalled us, a mystery of all mysteries, God began.
A miracle of all mysteries, strange, mysterious reversal of all
    the mysteries.
All the feelings, all the emotions that we should have for God,
God has had for us, he began by having them for us.
Strange reversal that accompanies all the mysteries,
And redoubles them, and enlarges them to infinity,
We must have confidence in God, my child, he has certainly
    had confidence in us.
He had the confidence to give us, to confide to us his only
    son.
(Alas alas for how we abused that confidence.)
Reversal of everything it is God who began.
It is God who put his trust in us, who had confidence in us.
Who has believed in us, who has had faith in us.
Will this confidence be misplaced, will it be said that this
    confidence has been misplaced.
God has had hope in us. He began. He hoped that the vilest
    of sinners,
That the lowliest of sinners would at least work a little
    toward his salvation,
Little and poorly as it might be.
That he would work on it a little.
He hoped in us, shall it be said that we do not hope in him.
God pinned his hope, his meagre hope on each of us, on the
    lowliest of sinners.
Shall it be said that we lowly sinners, that it is we who would
    not pin our hope on him.
God entrusted his son to us, alas alas, God has entrusted our
    salvation to us, the work for our salvation. He has given
    us the responsibility for his son and our salvation and thus
    for his very hope; and we would not put our hope in him.

Mystery of mysteries, having a bearing on the mysteries them-
    selves,
He has put his eternal hope in our hands, in our feeble hands,
In our transitory hands.
In our sinful hands.
And we sinners would not put our feeble hope
In his eternal hands.

The word of God is not a tangled skein.
It is a beautiful woolen yarn wound around a spindle.
As he spoke to us, so we must listen to him.
As he spoke to Moses.
As he spoke to us through Jesus.
As he spoke to us, just so we must understand him.

Now, my child, if this is the case, if it is thus that we must
    understand Jesus.
That we must understand God.
Literally.
Strictly, simply, fully, exactly, sanely.
In a down-to-earth way.
Then my child what a tremor, what a command of hope.
What a glimpse, what a thrill of hope.
How overwhelming.   The words are there.
There is nothing to argue about, what a glimpse into God's
    thought.
Into God's will.
Into God's intentions.
Abyss of hope, what a glimpse, what a flash, what a thunderbolt,
    what an avenue.
What an entrance.
Irrevocable words, what a glimpse into the very Hope of God.
God deigned to hope in us.

Revelation, what an incredible revelation. Sic non est, Even
    so it is not
Incredible hope, unlooked for hope. Even so it is not
Voluntas ante Patrem vestrum, the will of your Father
Qui in coelis est. In heaven.
Ut unus. That a single one
Of these little ones. De pusillis istis.
Pereat. Should perish.

And he spoke to them this parable, saying:
What man of you having a hundred sheep;
(According to Saint Luke;)
And losing one of them,
Does not leave the ninety-nine in the desert,
And go after that one,

Quae perierat, which WAS lost, which HAD perished, *

It was over.

Until he finds it?

And when he has found it,
He lays it upon his shoulders rejoicing;

(He places it) upon his shoulders.

And on coming home he calls together his friends and neighbors,
    saying to them:

*   Péguy here uses both auxiliaries, être and avoir, with périr,
a practice permissible only until the eighteenth century, in
order to emphasize the spiritual death of the lost soul.

"Rejoice with me, (be thankful), because I have found my sheep
   that was lost."

I say to you that, even so,
There will be as much joy in heaven
Over one sinner who repents,
As over ninety-nine just who have no need of repentance.

Now what is repentance, my child, what is there in repentance.
   What then is the secret virtue of repentance.
My child it is peculiar, it is strange, it is disturbing.
What then is so extraordinary about repentance?
How disturbing it is.
What is this virtue, this secret, what must there be that is
   so extraordinary,
About repentance,
   that this sinner,
That this one sinner should be worth a hundred souls, or
   ninety-nine anyway,
(To be exact),
That this sinner should be worth as much,
That this sinner, this one repentant sinner should be worth
   as much, should cause rejoicing, cause as much joy in heaven
   as the ninety-nine just who have no need of repentance.
And that this lost sheep should bring so much joy to the
   shepherd,
To the good shepherd,
That he leaves in the desert, in deserto, in the wilderness,
The ninety-nine who had not strayed.
Wherefore, what is this mystery then,
How can one be worth ninety-nine.
Are we not all children of God.   All on an equal footing.
Wherefore, how, why is one sheep worth ninety-nine sheep.
   And especially why is it precisely the one which has
   strayed, which had perished, which is worth precisely the

ninety-nine others, the ninety-nine which had not left the
   fold.
Why, what is this mystery, what is this secret, it is suspect,
   how, why, wherefore should one soul be worth ninety-nine
   souls, it is not fair.
All the same it is not fair when you come to think of it.
What is this little scheme.
It is precisely this soul that was lost, that had perished,
   which is worth as much, which causes as much joy in heaven
   as the ninety-nine others.
As those ninety-nine which had not gone astray.
   Not once.
Which had not been lost, which had not perished.
   Not once.
Which had held firm.
It is unfair. What is this idea, this new idea.
It is unfair. There is a soul (and it is precisely the one
   that had strayed), that is worth as much, that counts for as much,
   that causes as much rejoicing as the ninety-nine wretched
   ones that had remained steadfast.
Why; wherefore; how. One man weighs as heavily on God's scale
   as ninety-nine.
Weighs as heavily? Who weighs perhaps more heavily. In secret.
We can't tell. I am very much afraid. Secretly we have the
   impression that he weighs more heavily, when we read this
   parable.
There is a sinner then, let us say, who weighs at least as much
   as ninety-nine just.
Who even perhaps weighs more. We can't tell. Once we have
   encountered unfairness.
We can no longer calculate.
Let us say the word there is an unbeliever, it must be said,
   we must not be afraid of the word.
Who is worth more than a hundred, than ninety-nine faithful.
   What is this mystery.

What then could be the extraordinary virtue of repentance.

That would outstrip a hundredfold even fidelity.

We must not delude ourselves.   We very well know what repentance is.

A penitent is a man who is not very proud of himself.

Who is not very proud of what he has done.

Because what he has done, we must admit, is sinful.

A penitent is a man who is ashamed of himself and of his sin.

Of what he has done.

Who would like very much to burrow out of sight.

Above all he is a man who wishes he had not done it.

     Had never done it.

Who wishes to hide, to escape from the face of God.

And what too is that drachma that is worth nine drachmas, all
by itself.

How does it enter the picture.

And yet it is that one, and no other, it is that sheep, it is
that sinner, it is that penitent, it is that soul

That God, that Jesus carries back on his shoulders, forsaking
the others.

At any rate I mean (only) leaving them alone for a little
while.

Repentance, we know, is really not as splendid as all that.

It is not so radiant.

(It is true that God never leaves anyone.)

It is a shameful feeling, I mean a feeling of shame.

Of rightful and proper shame.

In short it is a shamefaced act.

Repentance is certainly not as brilliant as that.

     Well then.

Not only this penitent is worth as much as another, not only
is he worth as much as a just man, which would already be
hard to accept,

But he is worth ninety-nine of them, a hundred of them, the
whole flock.

So to speak.

If need be, you feel that he would be worth more and would be
　　more beloved
　　In the secret heart.
　　In the secret of the eternal heart. Well, then.
My child, my child, you know the answer. It is exactly that.
It is because the sheep had perished; and was found again.
Because it was dead; and lived again.
Because it was dead and is restored to life.

Since we must take everything literally, my child,
As Jesus was literally dead and is risen from the dead,
So this sheep was lost, so this sheep was dead,
So this soul was dead and by his own death it is risen from
　　the dead.

It made the very heart of God tremble.
With the tremor of fear and the tremor of hope.
With the very tremor of dread.
With the tremor of anxiety
Mortal anxiety.
And then, and so, and also
With what is linked to dread, to fear, to anxiety.
With what follows dread, fear, anxiety.
And what goes along with them, with what is linked to dread, to
　　fear, to anxiety
By an unbreakable link, by an indestructible bond,
Temporal and eternal, by an indestructible link
It made the heart of God tremble
With the very tremor of hope.
Into the very heart of God in introduced
Living hope.

There, my child, is the secret.   What a mystery there is.
What splendor, (hidden), what an unbelievable source of
   splendor there is in repentance.
In shamefaced repentance.   Secretly, publicly shamefaced and
   truly
Perhaps the most glorious of all.   The fact is that a man's
   repentance
Is the crowning of one of God's hopes.

This shamefaced repentance, ashamed and not knowing where to
   hide,
Where to hide its shamed face, its face red with shame, purple
   with shame,
Its head covered with ashes and earth,
As a sign of shame and repentance,
Where to hide its shame and its sin.
But God is not ashamed of it.
For the expectation of this repentance,
The anxious expectation, the hope of this repentance
Has made hope well up in the heart of God,
Has called forth a new feeling,
An almost unknown feeling, as it were, I know exactly what
   I mean,
Has caused to spring forth, to arise something like an unknown
   feeling in the very heart of God.
In his heart which is as it were renewed.
In the heart of God who is as it were renewed.   I understand,
   I know what I mean.
Of God who is eternally new.

And this very repentance
Was for him, in him, the crowning of a hope.

For all the others God loves in love.
But this sheep Jesus loved also in hope.

And all the others, all of us God loves in charity.
But one day God loved the sinner in hope.

We must take everything literally, my child.   God hoped and
    expected something from him.
God who is all, had something to hope for, from him, from this
    sinner. From this worthless creature.   From us.   He was put
    in the position, he put himself in the position, in the
    situation, of having to hope for, to expect something from
    this miserable sinner.

Such is the living strength of hope, my child,
The living strength, the promise, the life, that springs in
    the heart of hope
And that wells up in repentance.
In lowly repentance.

Such is the unique strength of sap in the heart of an oak.

We are all equally children of God, my child; on the same
    footing.

We must take everything literally, my child, the soul that
    called forth God's hope, that crowned God's hope
Dead as Jesus was dead (more truly dead than Jesus) by his death
    is risen from the dead.
(More truly dead than Jesus, infinitely more dead, eternally
    more dead, for it had died the eternal death).
Like Jesus it is risen from the dead.
And as we set all the bells ringing at Easter to celebrate
    the resurrection of Jesus,
Christ is risen!
So God for each soul saved rings out eternal Easter bells.

And he says: I told you so.

Strange reversal, singular reversal, the world is wrong side
    foremost.
Virtue of hope.
All the feelings we should have for God,
God began by having for us.
It is he who put himself in this position, in this situation,
    who was put in it, who allowed himself to be put in it,
    in the position, in the situation of beginning by having
    them for us.
Strange virtue of hope, strange mystery, hope is not a virtue
    like the others, but a virtue opposed to the others.
Hope takes the opposite view from all the others and leans
    so to speak on the others, on all the others.
And holds out against them. Against the virtues. Against all
    the mysteries.
Hope carries them along, so to speak, against the current.
Hope stems the current of the others.
She is not a slave, this child is a strong-minded person,
She answers back to her sisters; to all the virtues, to all the
    mysteries.
When they go downstream, she goes up, (she is right,)
When everything goes downstream she alone goes up and thus she
    doubles them, she increases them tenfold, she enlarges them
    to infinity.
It is she who has operated this reversal, this greatest re-
    versal of all,
(Perhaps it is the greatest thing she has done,)
(Who would have believed that so much power, such sovereign
    power was given to this little
Hope)
The reversal that in everything we should do for God
God forestalls us, and begins by doing it for us.
Everything that we should say to him, do for him, do in his
    behalf,
And all that we should have for God,
God begins by having for us.

He who loves puts himself, by that very fact,

By that fact alone, in a state of dependence,

He who loves becomes the slave of the one who is loved.

It is usual, it is the common lot.

It is inevitable.

He who loves falls into slavery, under the yoke of slavery.

He is dependent on the one he loves.

Yet it is that very situation, my child, into which God has put
himself by loving us.

God has deigned to hope in us, since he was willing to hope for,
to expect something from us.

Wretched stiuation, in return for what love,

Pledge, ransom of what love.

Strange reward. Which was within the conditions, in perfect
conformity with the nature of this love.

He has put himself in this strange reversed situation, in this
wretched situation in which it is he who expects something
from us, from the most miserable sinner.

Who hopes for something from the most miserable sinner.

And from us.

See where he has allowed himself to be led, by his great love,
see where he has placed himself, where he has been put,
anyway where he has allowed himself to be placed.

See what he has come to, where he is.

Where we should be he has put himself.

At the point, in the situation.

Where he has to fear, to hope for, anyway to expect something
from the vilest of men.

Where he is in the hands of the vilest of sinners.

(But is not the body of Jesus, in every church, in the hands
of the vilest of sinners.

At the mercy of the lowliest of soldiers.)

Where he has everything to fear from us.

(That he should have to fear anything is already too much, is
already everything,)

(No matter how little it may be, and in this case it is every-
    thing)
(No matter how little it may be, even if it were almost not at
    all, or not at all so to speak.)
Such is the situation in which God by the virtue of hope
In order to bring hope into play.
Has allowed himself to be put
In relation to the sinner.
He stands in fear of him, since he fears for him.
You understand, I am saying: God stands in fear of the sinner,
    since he fears for the sinner.
When you fear for someone, you stand in fear of him.
God has placed himself under this universal law.
Has submitted.
To this universal levelling.
He has suffered himself to be put under this universal law.
He has to await the convenience of the sinner.
He has placed himself on this footing.
He has to hope in the sinner, in us.
It is senseless, he has to hope that we will save ourselves.
He can do nothing without us.
He has to listen to our vagaries.
He has to wait until his Highness the sinner graciously deigns
    to give a little thought to his salvation.

That is the situation that God has created for himself.
He who loves becomes the slave of the beloved.
By the fact of loving.
He who loves becomes the slave of the beloved.
God did not wish to escape this universal law.
And because of his love he has become the slave of the sinner.

Reversal of creation, it is creation wrong side foremost.
The Creator is now dependent upon his creature.
He who is all has placed himself, has suffered himself to be

placed has allowed himself to be placed on this level.

He who is all depends upon, waits for, hopes for what is nothing.

He who is all powerful depends upon, waits for, hopes for what is powerless,

And at the same time powerful, alas, for everything has been handed to him,

Everything has been entrusted to him,

Everything has been given to him,

Everything has been placed in his hands, in his sinful hands,

Confidently,

Hopefully,

He has been given complete freedom.

Confidently.

He has been handed, he has been given his own salvation, the body of Jesus, the hope of God.

God has placed himself on this footing. As the most wretched creature was freely able

To strike freely the face of Jesus.

So the vilest creature can belie God's words

Or make them truthful.

Terrifying delegation of power.

Terrifying privilege, terrifying responsibility.

As Jesus world without end has placed his body

In the poorest churches

At the discretion of the lowliest of soldiers,

So God world without end has placed his hope

At the discretion of the lowliest of sinners.

As the victim surrenders himself into the hands of the executioner,

So Jesus has delivered himself into our hands.

As the victim is delivered to the executioner,

So Jesus has delivered himself to us.

As the prisoner is delivered to the prison guard,

So God has delivered himself to us.

As the lowliest of wretches was able to strike Jesus,
    And it had to be thus,
So the lowliest of sinners, a poor weakling.
The vilest of sinners can bring to naught, or to fulfilment
    One of God's hopes;
The vilest of sinners can uncrown, or crown
    One of God's hopes.

And it is of us that God expects
    The crowning or the uncrowning of one of his hopes.

Terrifying love, terrifying charity,
Terrifying hope, truly terrifying responsibility,
The Creator has need of his creation, has arranged to have
    need of his creation.
He can do nothing without it.
He is like a king who has simply surrendered the supreme
    power
To each of his subjects.
God has need of us, God has need of his creation.
He has so to speak thus condemned himself, condemned himself
    to this.
He needs us, he needs his creation.
He who is all needs what is nothing.
He who is all powerful needs what is powerless.
He has abdicated his full powers.
He who is all is nothing without him who is nothing.
He who is all powerful can do nothing without him who is
    powerless.
Just so young hope
Takes up, carries along, remakes,
Corrects all the mysteries
As she corrects all the virtues.

We can fail him.

Not respond to his call.

Not respond to his hope.   Default.   Be missing.   Not be there.

Terrifying power.

God's calculations can be upset by us.

The expectations, the foresight, the providence of God

Because of us can miscarry,

Through the fault of sinful man.

The counsels of God because of us can falter.

Terrifying freedom of man.

We can bring everything to naught.

We can be absent.

Not be there on the day we are called.

We can fail to respond to the call

(Except in the valley of Judgment.)

Terrifying favor.

We can fail God.

That is the situation in which he has placed himself,

The bad situation.

He has placed himself in the situtation of needing us.

What rashness.   What confidence.

Well placed, misplaced, that depends on us.

What hope, what obstinacy, what bias, what an unquenchable
   fund of hope.

In us.

What stripping, of himself, of his power.

What rashness.

What lack of sagacity, what want of foresight,

What improvidence

Of God.

We can default.

We can fail to appear.

We can be defaulting.

Terrifying favor, terrifying grace.

He who makes everything appeals to him who can make
Nothing.
He who makes everything needs him who makes nothing.
And as we set all the bells ringing at Easter,
In full peal,
In our poor, our triumphant churches,
In the sunshine and fine weather of Easter,
So God for each soul that is saved
Rings out a full peal of eternal Easter bells.
And says: Well, I wasn't mistaken.
I was right to have confidence in that boy.
He was a fine fellow. He came of good stock.
He had a good mother. He was a Frenchman.
I did right to trust him.
And we have our Sundays,
Our beautiful Sunday, Easter Sunday,
And Easter Monday,
And even Easter Tuesday, which is also a feast day,
So great is the feast.
(It is the feast of Saint Loup.)
But God has also his Sundays in heaven.
His Easter Sunday.
And he has also bells, when he wishes.

And also what is this about ten drachmas.
Which are as you might say ten francs minted in Paris.
What is this business about ten drachmas.
What is the connection with this drachma that is worth nine
    others.
Odd calculation, as if you said a franc minted in Paris which
    is worth nine other francs minted in Paris,
Nine others of the same kind. What odd arithmetic.
Yet it is thus, my child, that God's books are kept.

Thus were kept, my child, the books of Jesus. It is indisputable;
   there is no doubt that there are two strains of saints in
   heaven.
Two kinds of saints.
(Fortunately they get along well together.)
In the same way that the king's soldiers and captains
Are of various strains but are all Frenchmen.
And nevertheless comprise a single army.
And they are all soldiers (of the army) of the king, and the
   captains.
But they come from various provinces.
Or from a frontier. Some from one some from another.
Either from beyond the Loire or from this side of the Loire.
So, (and otherwise), to tell the truth there are two strains
   of saints in heaven.
Two temporal strains.
Two kinds of saints.
Everyone is sinful. Every man is a sinner. But there are two
   great strains, there are two recruiting sources.
There is twofold recruitment of the saints who are in heaven.
There are those who come, who emerge from the ranks of the just.
And there are those who emerge from the ranks of sinners.
And it is a difficult undertaking.
An impossible undertaking for man.
To know which are the greater saints.
So great are both strains.

There are two extractions (and yet, together, all equally saints
   in heaven. On the same footing) (Saints of God).
There are two extractions, those who come from the ranks of the
   just and those who come from the ranks of the sinners.
Those who have never aroused serious anxiety
And those who have aroused anxiety
Mortal anxiety.

Those who have not brought hope into play and those who have
brought hope into play.
Those for whom nothing has ever been feared, nothing serious
dreaded, and those who were almost despaired of, God preserve
us.
What a great combat.

Those we hear nothing about
And those about whom we have heard
The word
The mortal word.

There are two formations, two extractions, there are two strains
of saints in heaven.
The saints of God are graduated from two schools.
From the school of the just and from the school of the sinner.
From the wavering school of sin.
Fortunately it is always God who is the schoolmaster.

There are those from the ranks of the just and those from the
ranks of sinners.
And the fact is recognized.
Fortunately there is no jealousy in heaven.
On the contrary.
Since there is the communion of saints.
Fortunately they are not jealous of each other.   But all
together on the contrary are as close as the fingers of the
hand.
For all together they spend their time all the holy day together
plotting against God.
In the presence of God.
So that inch by inch, step by step

Justice may yield to Mercy.

They do violence to God.   Like good soldiers they fight inch
    by inch,
(They make war on justice
They are obliged to)
For the salvation of wavering souls.
They resist.   Moved, animated by hope,
They make bold with God.
(But also they have support, patronage, powerful protection.
What patrons, my children.
What (other) plot above them, encompassing their great plot,
Supporting their great plot.
What an advocate with God.
(Advocata nostra.)
For our patrons and saints, our patrons the saints
Themselves have two patrons.
Two saints.
One who is as far
(And seventy times as far) above them as they themselves are
Above us.
Who is for them what they are for us, and seventy times what
    they are for us,
Such is the folly of hope.
And encompassed, encouraged by this supernal plot,
By the protection of this supernal plot,
Fed on hope they resist like good soldiers.
They fight for every foothold, they defend the ground inch by
    inch.
One cannot imagine all that they do, all the things they think of
For the salvation of wavering souls.
Bit by bit they snatch
A soul in danger
From the kingdom of the damned.

So God has not wished

It has not pleased him

That there should be but one voice in the concert.

He did not deem it wise.

Nor to his liking.

He did not want to be praised by a single voice

By a single choir

Nor opposed.

But as in a country church there are several voices

Praising God.

For example men and women.

Or again men and children.

So in heaven he has deemed it wise.

And to his liking.

To be praised, to be hymned, to be opposed by two voices.

By two languages, by two choirs.

By the former just and by the former sinners.

So that inch by inch Justice might give way

    To Mercy.

And so that Mercy may advance

    And Mercy may win.

For if there were nothing but Justice and if Mercy did not

    enter into it,

Who would be saved.

Now what woman having ten pieces of silver

(It is again according to Saint Luke, my child,)

If she loses one drachma,

If she loses one of them,

Does not light a candle,

And sweep the house,

And search carefully,

Until she finds it?

And when she has found it,

103

She calls together her friends and her neighbors,
(They are always calling their friends and neighbors together
   in these parables,)
Saying:
Rejoice with me,
For I have found the drachma that I had lost.

Even so, I say to you,
There will be joy among the angels of God,
Over one sinner who repents.

There was a great procession; at the head of it advanced the
   three Similitudes;
   the parable of the lost sheep;
   the parable of the lost drachma;
   the parable of the lost child.

Now just as a child is more precious than a sheep,
And infinitely more precious than a drachma,
Just as a child is dearer to his father's heart,
(His father who is at the same time, who is already, first,
   who is primarily his shepherd,)
Dearer even than a sheep to the heart of the (good) shepherd,
By just so much the third Similitude,
By just so much the parable of the lost child
Is still more beautiful if possible and more precious,
Is still greater than the two preceding Similitudes,
Than the parable of the lost sheep,
And than the parable of the lost drachma.

All the parables are beautiful, my child, all the parables are
   great, all the parables are precious.

104

All the parables are the word and the Logos,
The word of God, the word of Jesus.
They are all equally, they are all jointly
The word of God, the word of Jesus.
On the same footing.
(God has put himself in the position, my child,
In the bad position
Of needing us.)
They all come equally from the heart, and they go straight
    to the heart,
They speak to the heart.
But among all the words, the three parables of hope
Advance,
And among all they are great and faithful, among all they are
    pious and affectionate, among all they are beautiful, among
    all they are precious and close to the heart.
Among all they are close to the heart of man, among all they
    are precious to the heart of man.
They have a certain place apart.
They have in them perhaps something that is not, that would
    not be in the others.
Perhaps they have in them a certain youthfulness, a certain
    childhood.
Unknown and unsuspected elsewhere.
Among all they are young, among all they are fresh, among all
    they are childlike, among all they are not outworn.
Unaged.
Not outworn, not aged.
Although they have served for thirteen or fourteen centuries,
    and for two thousand years, world without end, they are
    young as on the first day.
Fresh, innocent, ignorant,
Childlike as on the first day.
And for the thirteen hundred years that there have been Christians
    and the fourteen hundred years,

These three parables, (may God pardon us,)
Have had a secret place in the heart.
And may God pardon us as long as there are Christians,
So long in other words forever,
There will be world without end for these three parables
A secret place in the heart.

And all three are parables of hope.
Jointly.
Equally young, equally precious.
All three.
Sisters to each other like three quite young children.
Equally precious, equally secret.
Secretly loved.   Equally loved.
And as it were more personal than all the others.
As if responding to a more profound and personal voice.
But among all, among all three here is the third parable
    advancing.
And this one, my child, this third parable of hope,
Is not only new as on the first day.
Like the two others
The sister parables.
And for all time will be new,
Just as new until the last day.
But although this parable has served for fourteen hundred, for
    two thousand years,
And has been recounted to innumerable men,
(Since that first time of telling,)
To innumerable Christians,
Unless one had a heart of stone, my child, who could hear it
    without weeping.
For fourteen hundred, for two thousand years it has caused
    innumerable men to weep.
World without end.

Innumerable Christians.

In the heart of man it has touched a special point, a secret
point, a mysterious point.

(It has affected the heart.)

A point inaccessible to the others.

Some point that is more personal and more profound,

Innumerable men, since it has been serving, innumerable
Christians have wept over it.

(Unless they had hearts of stone.)

In centuries to come men will weep.

Only to think of it, only to see it who could,

Who would be able to contain his tears.

In centuries to come, in eternity men will weep over it;
because of it,

The faithful and unbelievers.

In the eternity until judgment.

Even at the judgment, on the day of judgment.   And

It is the saying of Jesus that has carried the farthest,
my child,

It has had the best luck

Temporal luck.   Eternal luck.

In the heart it has awakened a certain point of response

A special point.

It has also had special luck.

It is famous even among the ungodly.

Even there it has found a point of entry.

Perhaps alone it has remained planted in the heart of the
ungodly

Like a stab of love.

And he said: A certain man had two sons;

And for him who hears this for the hundredth time,

It is as if it were for the first time.

That he heard it.

A certain man had two sons.   It is beautiful in Luke.   It is
beautiful everywhere.

It is not only in Luke, it is everywhere.
It is beautiful on earth and in heaven.
It is beautiful everywhere.
At the very thought of it, a sob rises in your throat.
It is the saying of Jesus that has had the greatest repercussion
In the world.
That has resounded the farthest
In the world and in man.
In the heart of man.

In the faithful heart, in the unbeliever's heart.

What sensitive point of entry did it find
That no saying had found before,
That none has found (as surely) since.
What special point,
Still unsuspected,
Unfound since.
A point of pain, a point of distress, a point of hope.
A painful point, a point of anxiety.
A bruise in the heart of man.
A point that must not be pressed, a scar, the edge of a cica-
    trized wound.
Where one must not press.

A special point, special luck, special connecting strength.
A special attachment, a link between the faithful heart.
And the heart of the unbeliever.
All the parables are beautiful, my child, all the parables
    are great.
And especially the three parables of hope.
And besides all three parables of hope are young, my child.
But over this one hundreds and thousands of men have wept.
Hundreds of thousands of men.
Over this one.
Wracked by the same sobs, wept the same tears.

108

Faithful and unbelievers.

Prompting each other.

Convulsed by the same sobs

In a communion of tears.

Prostrated, doubled over, raised up by the same sobs, wept
  the same tears.

Faithful and unbelievers.

Shaken by the same sobs.

Wept like children.

A certain man had two sons.   Of all God's sayings

This one has wakened the farthest echo.

The most ancient echo.

The oldest, the newest.

The most recent.

In the faithful and in unbelievers.

Known and unknown.

A special echoing note.

It is the only echo that the sinner has never silenced in his
  heart.

When once this saying has bitten into his heart

No pleasure will henceforth efface

The trace of its teeth.

Such is this saying.   It is a saying that stays with you.

That follows you like a dog

That is beaten, but remains.

Like a mistreated dog that always comes back.

It remains faithful, it comes back like a faithful dog.

There is no use kicking and beating it.

It is faithful with a special

Fidelity,

Thus it goes with man in his greatest

Follies.

It teaches that all is not lost.

It is not the will of God

That a single one of these little ones should perish.

It is a faithful dog

That bites and licks you

And both actions restrain

The uncertain heart.

When the sinner moves away from God, my child,

As he moves away, as he sinks into lost lands, as he becomes
    lost

He throws down by the side of the road, among the brambles
    and the stones

As useless and encumbering and annoying his most precious
    possessions.   His most sacred possessions.

The word of God, the purest treasures.

But there is one saying of God that he will not throw away.

A saying which every man has wept over so many times.

And he is like the others, he too has wept.

There is one treasure of God, when the sinner moves away

Into the growing shadows.

When the lengthening

Shadows

Veil his eyes there is one treasure of God that he will not
    throw away among the brambles by the side of the road

For it is a mystery that follows, it is a saying that follows

Into the greatest

Estrangement.

One need not be concerned with it, with bearing it.

   For it

Is concerned with you and with being borne and with your
    bearing it.

It follows, it is a saying that continues, it is a treasure
    that goes with you.

The other sayings of God do not dare to accompany man

In his greatest

Follies.

But truly this one is shameless.

It holds man by the heart, at a point it knows and does not
    let him go.

It is not afraid.   It is not ashamed.

And no matter how far away man goes, the man who is being lost,

In no matter what country

In no matter what darkness,

Far from home, far from the heart,

And no matter into what shadows he sinks,

Shadows that veil his eyes,

Always a spark keeps watch, always a flame keeps watch, a tongue
of flame.

Always a light keeps watch and will never be put under a bushel.
   Always a lamp.

Always a stab of pain sears.   A certain man had two sons.
   A stab that he recognizes easily.

In the false tranquillity a stab of anxiety, a stab of hope.
   All the other words of God are modest.   They do not dare
   to accompany man into the shame of sin.

They are not forward enough.

In the heart, in the shame of the heart.

But this saying in truth is not ashamed.

You could say that it is not at all shy.

It is like a little sister of charity who is not afraid to
   handle a sick or a poor person.

It has so to speak

And even really challenged the sinner.

It has said to him: Wherever you go, I shall go.

You will see.

With me you'll have no peace.

I shall not leave you in peace.

And it is true, and he very well knows it.   And in his heart
   he loves his persecutor.

At the bottom of his heart, very secretly.

For in his heart of hearts, in the depths of his shame and his
   sin he prefers not to have peace.   It reassures him a little.

A painful point remains, a point of thought, a point of anxiety.

A bud of hope.
One spark will not be extinguished and it is
   the third Parable,
the terce saying of hope.   <u>A certain man had two sons.</u>

There was a great procession.   At its head the three Simi-
   litudes
were advancing.   Faith, said God, is not tricky.
Everybody believes.   I should like to see how they could do
   otherwise.
Yes, I should like to see how they could manage not to
   believe.
How they would go about it.
I burst forth so strikingly in my creation.
Even in the sea's abysses and in the briny depths.
In the depths of the sea.
In the flashes of lightening and the thunder of a stormy sky,
Of a heavy laden sky,
Which are like a cut in the sky.
A zigzag cut.
And in the reverberation of the thunder which is a sundering
   of the sky.
And in the rolling of distant thunder.
In the rolling and reverberation of thunder
And in the beautiful days when there is no breath of wind
In May.

Unless they are blind how could they not see me.
Charity, said God, is not tricky.   It does not surprise me
   either.
These poor children are so unhappy that unless they have hearts
   of stone
How could they help loving their brothers.
How could they help loving each other.

But hope, said God, (a certain man had two sons), that these
  poor children should see every day how things go.
And every day believe that things will be better tomorrow morning
Precisely tomorrow morning.
Every day since days began.
And that a better day will dawn.
Every morning when they get up they believe that the day will
  be good.
That day.
And every evening when they go to bed they believe that to-
  morrow.
Precisely tomorrow, the following day
Will be a good day.
After so long a time since days began.
And since misfortune is their lot.
That all the evidence to the contrary does not count, so much
  evidence that they see precisely every day.
That the evidence is of no consequence, does not stop them,
  that the evidence of every day,
As measureless as the days,
Measureless in the measureless day that the evidence
Does not disabuse them of this idea, of this absurd conviction
That today will be a better day,
Another day, a new day, a fresh day, a brand new day.
A dawning day,
Well washed, a day in short, a good day,
Finally,
A day different from the others,
After so many others that were all alike,
That they have even forgotten.
Forgotten as soon as they were over.
Forgotten as soon as they were lived.
Forgotten as soon as they were received.
That they should believe that this morning, oh well, things
  will be all right.

Things will go well.

That they should believe in spite of everything, that this
   morning, all will be well,

That confounds me.

That is beyond me.

And I cannot get over it.

And my grace must be so great.

And that they instantly forget the bad days.

Continually.   Immediately.

Almost before they happen.   Almost in advance.

That they stifle the memory of the bad days in advance so to
   speak

That they absorb the bad days almost before they are passed.

Before they have rolled by.

Before they have elapsed.

Before they have closed.

Like burning earth that absorbs the harshness of heaven.

That they absorb the bad days so to speak more quickly than the
   bad days can be rained upon them.

The bad days that rain upon them like an autumn rain.

Like a grey rain, like an inexhaustible rain,

Pitilessly

Falling, coming down from a sky that is blotted out

Rather than grey.

Like an inexhaustible slanting rain.

That they absorb all that falls upon them as does the good
   land of Lorraine,

As healthy and productive earth,

In exactly the right condition, very light,

Drinks up all that falls and does not allow itself to be
   flooded by marshes and swamps.

And ponds and pools and swamps full of mud and slime,

And by the soul's sloughs and sticky gummy plants.

And slimy gluey creatures.

But on the contrary out of all that falls upon them and out
   of the countless rains and the countless bad days
Immediately, instantly, almost in advance that they should produce
   flowing water,
Living water, clear water, fresh water.
Beautiful limpid water.
Pure water that gushes forth and flows over these meadows
To the banks of the Meuse.
Beautiful water of Lorraine, a soul of fine water and the very
   fountain of hope.
That it should be precisely from this material, from these
   countless bad days that rain and rain upon them
That they produce, that they put forth, that they cause to gush
   forth this fountain of hope.
This measureless fountain and this measureless river.
The greatest of all my rivers.
The only great one.
That is what I admire, and I know what I'm talking about.
I know my creation.   And the work of the Six Days.
And the repose of the Seventh.
That is what surprises me.   And yet I am not easily surprised.
I am so old.   I have seen so much.   I have done so much.
That is what is beyond me and I cannot get over it.
My grace has to be so great.

The bad days rain down; unhurriedly; tirelessly; hour after
   hour, day after day.
   The bad days rain down.
And with all the water that slips tirelessly from the sky,
   (from the sky that they could call bad,)
With all this water that falls to earth, with all this slanting
   rain,
   (Others would make marshes and swamps full of fever and
   peopled with dirty disgusting creatures.)
But they, the good soil, my light well-tilled soil,
Well prepared.

My good soil of souls, well tilled by my Son for centuries
   and centuries,
They, my good healthy soil of Lorraine, collect all the rain
   that falls.
And, for a wonder, they do not make of it marshes and mud and
   slime.
And algae and hart's-tongue and queer plants.
But, for a wonder, it is this very water that they collect
   and that does not trouble them.
Because, for a wonder, it is from this very water that they
   produce the fountain.

It is this water, the same water that flows through the meadows.
It is the same pure water that climbs up the stalks of wheat
   for the Bread.
It is the same pure water that climbs up the vine-shoots for
   the Wine.
It is the same pure water that climbs up to the buds and the
   budding,
In both Laws.
It is the same water, collected, the same water pure,
   purified, that goes around the world.
And returns, reappears, having flowed around my whole creation.
It is the same collected water that gushes forth, that springs
   forth.
In the new fountain, in the young spring.
In the springing and respringing of hope.

Truly, said God, my Son has made me some very good gardeners
During the fourteen centuries that he has been peopling this
   earth with souls.
During the fourteen centuries that my Son has been tilling and
   cultivating this land,

116

He has made me some very good tillers and cultivators.

And harvesters and vine-growers.   Some expert vine-growers.

The bad days that rain and rain and that everywhere else would
    poison the entire country.

Whole nations, whole peoples, whole creations.

These rains that everywhere else would flood,

Would muddy the arable land with filthy slime,

Would drown every shoot and bud

Under kelp and slimy worms.

All the bad days that rain and rain

Everywhere else would inundate and contaminate

The good arable land,

Would engulf, would envelop my whole creation

In pestilence.

But here, said God, in the sweet land of France, my noblest
    creation,

In this pure Lorraine,

Here are good gardeners.

They are accomplished old gardeners, expert gardeners for the
    fourteen centuries that they have been following the lessons
    of my Son.

They have channeled everything, hoed everything in the gardens
    of the soul.

The water that serves for flooding, for poisoning (laughing)
    they use for watering.

My Son's people, a people full of grace, eternally filled with
    youth and grace.

The very waters of heaven you divert; for your marvellous
    gardens.

My very anger you divert; for your marvellous mysterious
    gardens.

The very pestilences you divert and they do not touch you and
    they only serve you as fertilizer

For your marvellous mysterious gardens.

O people you have learned well the lessons of my Son.

Who was a great Gardener.

People secretly loved it is you who have succeeded best.

Gardening people pure water will always nourish your lands.

Peoples; people who do not retreat before any pestilence.

O my people of France, O my people of Lorraine.   Pure people,
   healthy people, gardening people.

Tilling and cultivating people.

People who till most deeply

Soil and souls.

Your waters will always be living waters.

And your springs will always be gushing fountains.

Your streams will always be flowing water and rivers,

And the secret springs in your mysterious,

Your marvellous, your sorrowful gardens.

Flowing water, pure water will always nourish your meadows.

Pure water will always climb up your Wheat.

Pure, rare, abundant, precious water will always climb up your
   Vines.

People who make the Bread, people who make the Wine.

O my land of Lorraine, O my land of France,

People who follow the best, who have best learned the lessons
   of my Son.

People who work with little Hope.

That springs up everywhere in this land.

And in the mysterious,

The marvellous, the sorrowful gardens of souls

Gardening people who have grown the most beautiful flowers

Of holiness

By the grace of this little Hope.

People who repulse pestilence

With order.   With cleanliness, with honesty; with light.

With a virtue that is in you, with a clean virtue, with a
   special virtue.

Gardening people, who plow and harrow,

Who spade and rake,

Who hoe creation itself.

And I say it, said God, I declare it: Nothing is as profound
as tilling.

And nothing in my creation is as great

As these beautiful tidy gardens of souls such as the French make.

All the wild beauties of the world, you may believe me, who
should know better than I,

All the wild beauties of the world are not worth one beautiful
French garden.

For that is where you find the most soul and the most creation.

That is where there is soul.

Mysterious gardens, marvellous gardens,

Sorrowful gardens of French souls.

All the wild beauties of the world are not worth one beautiful
French garden.

Seemly, modest, tidy.

That is where I have plucked the most beautiful souls.

All the wild beauties of the world are not worth a beautiful
arrangement.

Honest people, gardening people it is they who grow the most
beautiful souls

Of holiness.

Sorrowful gardens where souls have grown

That suffered the most painful martyrdom

Without disturbing the arrangement

And that is what is difficult; that is what is rare

The most harrowing martyrdom

Without disturbing the arrangement.

And I know what thet costs.

Sorrowful gardens, where souls have grown that I have plucked

In their sorrow.

All the wild beauties of the world are not worth a good presby-
tery garden.

With its turnsoles,

That the children call sunflowers.

The good garden of a priest.

Calm and restful.

That is where I have plucked my most beautiful silent

Souls.

The heathen will say that this garden is not great and is not
profound.

But I know, (said God), that nothing is as great as order and
nothing as profound as tilling

French tilling.

Honest people, full of youth,

Full of my youth and my grace.

The waters of heaven do not intimidate you.

They do not bother you, you divert the waters of heaven.

The bad days rain and rain upon you, and do not corrupt you.

On the contrary, people who purify everything.

France my eldest daughter.

You do not allow the bad days to engender corruption and
pestilence.

Turbid waters, stagnant waters,

You do not allow the bad days to engender stagnant water.

Glairy water.

But you, a gardening people, make of them beautiful streams of
living water

That nourish the most beautiful gardens

There have ever been in the world.

That nourish the gardens of my grace, the eternal gardens.

I know, said God, how long Frenchmen can keep silent.

So as not to disturb a plan.

I know to what lengths Frenchmen can go so as not to disturb an
arrangement.

And that they suffer inwardly, and how greatly,

What trials they bear, unshaken,

Like a fine bridge, like a well-built vault.

What sacrifices they bring to me, (in secret), no sacrifice
is as profound

As French tilling.
Pure water, running water, flowing water rises
In the stalks of the law of Bread.
Running water, flowing water rises, rare water
In the vine-shoots of the law of Wine.
Water of Lorraine, water of France, rises in the budding
Of both laws.

Frenchmen, said God, it is you who invented these beautiful
    gardens of souls.
I know what marvellous flowers grow in your mysterious gardens.
I know what trials
You bear tirelessly.
I know what flowers and what fruit you bring me in secret.
It is you who invented the garden.
The others make only monstrosities.
You are he who designs the King's garden.
So I say to you truly it is you who will be my gardeners in
    the sight of God.
It is you who will design my gardens in Paradise.

There must have been something, said God, between our Frenchmen
    and little Hope.
They have such marvellous success.

Laborious people, people of the deepest tilling.
They are not ones to stagnate and sink in the marshes of
    laziness.
In the stagnant ponds, in the ditches, in the stagnating ponds.
Wallowing in the mud of laziness.
Wallowing in despair.
Wallowing in the mud of sin.
Alert people, gardening people with whom the bad days
Do not settle, do not extravasate

Into stagnating ponds but the market-gardeners
Make of the very marshes the most beautiful gardens.
They grow the most beautiful vegetables, the most beautiful
    fruit.
And their souls are always flowing water living water.
And their work is always flowing water.
And their prayers, I know, are always flowing water.

Strange people, it must be, said God, that there was some
    intimacy.
Some dealing.
That some deal has been arranged between these people and little
    Hope.
They succeed too well for it to be otherwise.
And they are the only ones who do succeed.
They must have arranged a sort of adoption between them.
They have adopted hope and hope has adopted them.
Not certainly in the way that a father adopts a daughter and
    a daughter adopts a father.
But more familiarly.
With a more familiar intimacy.
They are on the same terms with her, (I know the families
Of men), as an uncle with his niece
In the homes where there is an uncle a certain freedom exists
Between him and the children
A familiarity
That the father can never have.
A connivance, a secret understanding, never mentioned.
But they do not need to mention it.
They do not need to acknowledge it to each other.
To see it.
It is there.
The father is the parent, his brow is furrowed, his eyes
    scowling, he is burdened with the direct responsibility.
And the children feel this.
He is above them.

And the children feel this.

The tie between father and son is a sacred tie, one that lies
heavy, a direct tie.

And the children feel this.

The uncle has a freedom, (with age and experience at the same
time), he does whatever he wants, for the children

He represents all the amusement of life.

The children know it.   Only with him

Is the conversation amusing, only with him are the games
amusing.

He only is familiar.

This is the sort of relationship that the French have established
with little Hope.

She is happy only with them.

She listens to all their conversation.   There is none but theirs.

Whatever they say is good.   She identifies herself with them.

Only their stories are good.   She stays on their knees.   She
asks for each story twenty times.

That is the relationship that the French have established with
the child Hope.

Strange people for whom all water is a living spring.

All water that falls becomes flowing water.

By the ministry of hope.

All water, all impure water becomes for them drinkable water.

The impure water often makes them ill.

The impure water never poisons them.

They drink it all with impunity.

Because of this relationship they have with little Hope.

One wonders, one asks: But how can it be

That the fountain of Hope flows eternally,

Gushes eternally, springs eternally,

Flows eternally,

Eternally young, eternally pure.

Eternally fresh, eternally flowing.

Eternally living.   Where does this child get so much pure
   limpid water.
So much gushing and so much springing.
Does she create them?   As needed?
 - No, said God, only I create.
 - Then where does she get all the water.
For this gushing fountain.
How is it that this eternal fountain
Gushes eternally
That this eternal spring
Springs eternally.
There must be a secret.
Some mystery.
For this spring to remain eternally untroubled by the heavy
   torrential rains of autumn.
For it never to dry up in the burning heat of July.
 - Good folk, said God, it is not tricky.
Its mystery is not tricky.
And its secret is not difficult.
If it were with pure water that she tried to make pure springs,
Springs of pure water,
She would never find enough, in my whole creation.
For there is not very much.
But it is precisely with impure water that she makes her springs
   of pure water.
And that is why she never lacks.

But that is also why she is Hope.

Now how she goes about making pure water from impure water,
Young water from old water,

Young days from old days.
New water from used water.

Springs from old water.
Fresh souls from old souls.

Springs of soul from old soul.
Cool water from tepid water.

Woe to him of little faith.

Young mornings from old evenings.
Clear souls from troubled souls.

Clear water from troubled water.
Childlike souls from used souls.
Dawning souls from setting souls.
Flowing souls from stagnant souls.

How she succeeds, how she goes about it,
That, my children, is my secret.
Because I am her Father.

New souls from souls that have already been used.
New days from days that have already been used.

Limpid souls from troubled souls.
Rising souls from setting souls.
Limpid days from troubled days.

If it were from limpid days that she made limpid days.
If it were from souls, from clear water that she made springs.
From clear water that she made clear water.
If it were from pure soul that she made pure soul,
My word, that would not be tricky.   Anybody could do the same.
    And there would be no secret.
But it is from polluted water, old water, insipid water.

But it is from impure soul that she makes a pure soul and that
   is the finest secret there is in the garden of the world.

If it were from pure water that she made pure water, she knows
   what she is doing, she is tricky.
If it were from pure water that she made gush forth a spring
   of pure water,
She would run short of it at once.
She is not so stupid, she knows very well that she would run
   short of it at once.

But it is from impure water that she makes an eternal spring.
   She knows that she will never run short.
The eternal fountain of my grace itself.
   She knows that she will never run short.
And my grace has to be so great.
It is with troubled water that she makes her fountains.
   Thus she will never run short.
Her perfectly pure fountains.
It is with an impure day that she makes the pure day.
   She will never run short.
It is with impure soul that she makes the pure soul.
   She will never run short.

There was a great procession.   It was the Corpus Christi
   procession.   The Holy Sacrament was being carried.   So
   at the head marched
The three Theologals.   Look, said God, how the little one is
   marching.
Just take a look at her.
The others, the other two, are walking like grown-ups, her
   two big sisters.   They know where they are.   They are proper.

126

They know that they are in a procession.

Above all a Corpus Christi procession.

Where the Holy Sacrament is being carried.

They know what a procession is.

And that they are in the procession, at the head of the
procession.

They are going in procession.   They behave well.

They move forward like grown-ups.

Serious grown-ups.   Who are always a little tired.

But she is never tired.   Just take a look
At how she is walking.

She goes ahead twenty times, like a puppy, she comes back, she
starts off again, she covers the distance twenty times.

She plays with the garlands of the procession.

She plays with the flowers and leaves

As if they were not sacred garlands.

She would play at jumping over the freshly cut, freshly
gathered

Foliage strewn about.

She listens to nothing.   She does not stay still at the stations.

She would like to be moving all the time.   Going forward.

Jumping.   Dancing.   She is happy.

O people, gardening people, who grow the roses of France

For the processions.

Gardeners of the king, gardeners of flowers and fruit,
gardeners of souls

O people, you are my gardeners.

Gardeners in the orchard, gardeners in the vegetable patch,
gardeners in the garden.

Gardeners even in the field.

Gardening people, honest people, clean people.

Upright people.

Your forests are cleaner even than the king's park.

Your (wildest) woods are cleaner than the king's orchard.

Your fields and valleys are cleaner than the king's garden.

In your largest fields I do not see a single weed.

Laborious people I look in vain, your fields are as pure as
a fine garden.
And your distant valleys that curve gently.
Filled with fruitfulness. Developing in your care. With secret
hollows.
Diligent people, the plow and the harrow and the roller, the
spade and the rake and the pickaxe and the hoe and the dibble
and string
Are not idle in your hands.
Do not loaf in your hands.
You are not afraid of touching them. You do not look at them
solemnly from a distance.
But of the plow, the harrow and the roller, the shovel, the
pickaxe, the spade and the hoe
You make good honest workers, tools of respectable men.
You are not afraid to approach them.
The palm of your hand polishes the handle of the tool, gives
its wood a fine gloss.
The tool's handle polishes the palm of your hand, gives its
leathery surface a fine gloss,
A yellow gloss.
Of your tools you make agile tools. Diligent tools. Honest
tools.
Tools that move quickly. And they are well helved.
First people, you are first in the kichen-garden,
First in the orchard. First in the garden.
First in the fields.
You are the only ones in all that.
You grow the finest vegetables and the finest fruit.
You gather the finest vegetables and the finest fruit.
You even gather the finest leaves.
You strew the finest foliage.
At the feet of the three Theologals.
At the grave feet of my daughter Faith you strew the finest
and greatest foliage

That is strewn.

At the bleeding feet of my fervent daughter Charity you lay the
    finest, the tenderest foliage
That is strewn
The coolest to her feet.
So cool that the freshness of it rises to your heart and right
To your dry lips.   Cool foliage
That is like balm to the aching heart.
For it is like balm to the painful feet
To the bleeding feet, to the blood-stained feet.   At the feet
    of Cinderella, of my little child Hope
You cast, people, the most spouting foliage
That is strewn.   Streets filled with foliage.   And at the feet
    of great Processions,
People, and at the feet of the great Holy Sacrament,
At the feet of the Highest, my people you scatter the roses
    of France.
At the feet of the great Processions people you lay
The greatest Flowers, the greatest Leaves
The finest, the greatest flowers of the carnal earth.
The greatest flowers of the world,
The terrestrial world.
The greatest flowers of earth and soul
The greatest flowers of strain and earth.
Nourished with water.
And with earth.
People, you have made a garden of your kingdom.
Gardener of the king.   Kingdom of the king.
People you have made a garden of your fields.
People you cast without counting at the feet of the Highest
Flowers and souls,
Knowing that there will always be flowers and souls.
That you will always cultivate them.
People, people, the only ones who never bargain with me,
People of the king, people king, I tell you, I shall take you

to the king.

I too am king.   I shall take you to the king for my kingdom.

Gardener of the king, I shall take you to the king

On the day of the Coronation

To design my gardens

In my kingdom of Paradise.

People, I shall make you my gardening people.

People who have a taste for the string and the dibble,

And you will make me some of those beautiful roses of France,

Some of those beautiful white lilies of France

Those straight-stemmed lilies.

People of nurserymen, country of rose gardens, punctilious
    people.

Patient people, who have the patience (and the taste) for weeding,

People who never cease to weed.   Faster and more constant and
    more vigorous than nature itself.

More bent toward earth, more bowed, more bent on weeding, you
    who move faster and are more constant and more vigorous in
    weeding.

Than the weeds in growing (and that is saying a lot)

Than evil nature itself in growing weeds

People who are more efficient at pulling weeds than evil nature
    is at growing them.

(And that is saying a lot.   I ought to know.)

People more stubborn, more patient, more persevering than evil
    nature itself

When I look at your fields, I look in vain for a weed.

Not a thistle for the donkeys.   Nor that cockle that my Son
    called tares

And often used in his similitudes.   A certain man had two sons.

And that the rest of you call cockles and couch-grass.

Hard-working people, when I look at your harvests

I look in vain for that frightful disease.

When the wheat is sick.   And especially the rye.

130

That ergot, that blight of the rye, that frightful
Dry rot that poisons
That dares to poison the very bread.

When I look at your fields, Frenchmen,
I wish that you could also in the same way clear
Your souls
Of all those weeds of sin.
Of that blight, of that hatefulness that gnaws
The Eternal Bread.

People who cast armfuls
Of the beautiful straight-stemmed lilies of France,
Laid down,
Strewn,
Cut down.
At the feet of the Holiest and the Immaculate One.

See this child, said God, how she walks.
She would skip rope in a procession.
She would march, she would advance by skipping rope, for a bet.
So happy is she
(She alone of them all)
And so sure is she of never getting tired.
Children walk exactly like puppies.
(Besides they also play like puppies)
When a puppy takes a walk with his masters
He comes and goes. He sets forth and comes back. He starts
     forward and returns.
He covers the road twenty times.
Twenty times the distance.
The truth is that he is not going anywhere.
It is his masters who are going somewhere.
He has no destination.

What interests him is just making the trip.

It is the same with children.   When you make a trip with your
children

When you do an errand

Or when you go to mass or vespers with your children

Or to recite the rosary

Or between mass and vespeı s when you go for a walk with your
children

They trot in front of you like puppies.   They advance and
retreat.   They go and come.   They play.   They jump.

They cover the distance twenty times.

The truth is they are not going anywhere.

It does not interest them to go anywhere.

They have no destination.

It is the grown-ups who are going somewhere

The grown-ups, Faith and Charity

It is the parents who are going somewhere.

To mass, to vespers, to recite the rosary.

To the river, to the forest.

To the fields, to the woods, to work.

The grown-ups who are endeavoring, who are straining to get
somewhere

Or who are even going somewhere for a walk.

But what interests the children is just making the trip.

Coming and going and jumping.   Using up the road with their
legs.

Never having enough of it.   And feeling their legs grow.

They drink up the road.   They are thirsty for the road.   They
never have enough of it.

They are stronger than the road.   They are stronger than
fatigue.

They never have enough of it (Hope is like that).   They run
faster than the road.

They are not going, they are not running in order to arrive.
They arrive for the running.   They arrive for the going.   Hope

is like that.   They do not spare their steps.   The idea does
not occur to them.
To spare anything at all.
It is grown-ups who are sparing,
Alas they are compelled to be sparing.   But the child Hope
Never spares anything.
It is parents who are sparing.   A sorry virtue, alas, that
they should make a virtue of it.
They are compelled to.   Steady as my daughter Faith is,
Firm as a rock, she is compelled to be sparing.
Fervent as my daughter Charity is
Glowing like a fine wood fire
That warms the poor man by the hearth
The poor man and the child and the starving,
She is compelled to be sparing.
Only the child Hope
Alone spares nothing.
She does not spare her steps, the little minx, she does not
spare ours.
As she does not spare the flowers and leaves for great pro-
cessions,
And the roses of France and the beautiful lilies of France,
The straight-stemmed lilies,
So in the little and the long procession, in the difficult
procession of life she spares nothing
Neither her steps nor ours,
In the ordinary, gray, common procession
Of every day
(For every day is not Corpus Christi.)
She does not spare her steps, and since she treats us as she
treats herself,
She does not spare ours either.
She does not spare herself; and likewise, she does not spare
others either.
She makes us begin the same thing twenty times over.
She makes us return twenty times to the same place.

133

Which is generally a place of disappointment
(Earthly disappointment.)
She does not care. She is like a child. She is a child.
She does not care if she deceives grown-ups.
Earthly wisdom is not her business.
She does not calculate as we do.
She calculates, or rather she does not calculate, she counts
    (without noticing) as a child does.
Like someone who has his whole life before him.
She does not care if she deceives us.
She believes, she expects us to be like her.
She does not spare our troubles. Nor our pain.
    She expects
Us to have all our life before us.
How wrong she is. How right she is
For have we not all of Life before us.
The only life that counts. All of life Eternal.
And has not the old man as much life before him as the child
    in the cradle.
If not more. Since for the child in the cradle eternal Life,
The only life that counts, is masked by this wretched life
That he has to face. First. Right before him. This wretched
    earthly life.
That he must traverse. He has to pass through this wretched
    earthly life
Before arriving, before attaining, in order to attain Life
The only life that counts. But the old man is lucky.
He has carefully put behind him this wretched life
Which masked for him eternal Life.
Now he is free. He has put behind him what was before.
He sees clearly. He is old. Between him and life there is
    no longer anything. He is at the verge of light.
He is on the very brink. He is full of years. He is on the
    verge of eternal life.
It is right to say that old men are careful.
Just as that child was right to expect

Us to be like her.
Us to have all our life before us.
We have as much as she.   What does it matter to her
If she makes us take the same trip twenty times.
She is right.   What is important
(If she makes us go twenty times to the same place
Which is generally a place of disappointment,
Earthly disappointment) what is important
Is not going here or there, is not going to some place,
Arriving at some place,
Some earthly place.   It is going, always going, and (on the
    contrary) not arriving.
It is going in our limited way in the little procession of
    ordinary days,
The great procession toward salvation: The days go in procession
And we go in procession in the days.   What is important
Is the going.   To be always going.   That counts.   And how we go.
It is the road we take.   It is the way itself.
    And how we take it.
You go twenty times over the same earthly road.
    To come twenty times to the end.
And twenty times you come to, you gain, you reach
Painfully, laboriously, with difficulty,
Sorrowfully
The same place of disappointment,
Earthly disappointment.
And you say: That little Hope has deceived me again.
I ought not to have trusted her.   This is the twentieth time
    that she has deceived me.
(Earthly) wisdom is not her strong point.
I shall never believe her again.   (You will believe her
    again, you will always believe her.)
I shall never be caught again. - Fools that you are.
What matters that place where you wanted to go.
Where you thought you were going.

Look, you are not children, you knew very well
That the place where you were going would be a place of
    disappointment,
Earthly disappointment.   That it was such in advance.   Then
    why did you go there.
Since you understand very well the trickery
Of little Hope.
Why do you always follow that deceitful child.
Why do you always give in to the child's trickery.
And the twentieth time more firstly than the first time.
Why do you always accept it willingly.
And the twentieth time more readily than the first time.
The fact is that in your heart you very well know what she is.
What she does.   And that she deceives us
Twenty times.
Because she is the only one who does not deceive us.
    And that she disappoints us
Twenty times
All our lives
Because she is the only one who does not disappoint us
For Life.
And thus she is the only one who does not disappoint us.
For those twenty times that she makes us retread the same road
On earth in human wisdom are twenty times that are doubled
That are repeated, that are the same
That are twenty times vain, that are superposed
Because they led by the same route
To the same place, because it was the same route.   But in the
    wisdom of God
Nothing is ever nothing.   All is new.   All is otherwise.
All is different.
In the sight of God nothing is repeated.
Those twenty times that she made us take the same route to
    arrive at the same point
Of vanity.

In human sight it is the same point, it is the same route,
   they are the same twenty times.
But that is what is deceiving.
That is the false calculation and the false reckoning,
Being the human reckoning.
And here is what is not deceiving: Those twenty times are not
   the same time. If those twenty times are twenty times of
   trial and if this road is a road of holiness
On the same road the second time doubles the first
And the third triples it and the twentieth multiplies it twenty-
   fold.
What does it matter if one arrives here or there, and
   always at the same place
Which is a place of disappointment.
It is the route that is important, and what route one takes
   and being on it what one does,
How one does it.
It is the trip alone that is important.
If the road is a way of holiness
In the sight of God, a way of trials
He who has trod it twice is twice as holy
In the sight of God and he who has trod it thrice
Three times holier and he who has trod it
Twenty times is twenty times holier. That is the way God
   reckons.
That is the way God sees it.
The second time over the road is no longer the same.
Every day, you say, every day is alike
On earth, all days are the same day.
Starting with the same mornings they bring you to the same
   evenings.
But they do not lead you to the same eternal evenings.
All the days, you say, are alike. - Yes, all earthly days.
But set your minds at rest, children, they in no wise resemble
The last day, which is unlike all others.
All the days, you say, are repeated.

No, they are added
To the eternal treasury of days.
Each day's bread to the bread of the day before.
Each day's suffering
(Even though it would repeat the suffering of the day before).
To the eternal treasury of suffering.
Each day's prayer
(Even though it would repeat the prayer of the day before)
To the eternal treasury of prayers.
Each day's merit
(Even though it would repeat the merit of the day before)
To the eternal treasury of merit.
On earth everything is repeated.   In the same matter.   But
    in heaven everything counts
And everything is added up.   Each day's grace
(Even though it repeats the grace of the day before)
To the eternal treasury of grace.   And that is why only
    young Hope
Is sparing of nothing.   When Jesus was working in his father's
    shop
Every day he relived the same day.
There was not a single incident
Except once.
Yet it is the stuff, in these same days,
It is the fabric of these same workdays
That constitutes, that eternally constitutes
The admirable Life of Jesus before his preaching
His private life
His perfect life, his model life.
The one he offers as an example, as an inimitable Model to
    imitate
To everyone, with no exceptions, leaving only to a few
To a few rare chosen ones (and still it is in addition and
    not an alternative)
The examples of his public life to imitate

138

The inimitable models of his Preaching
Of his Passion and his Death.
(And his Resurrection.)
Similarly, together with him, in imitation of him
On earth, on our earthly roads our steps efface our steps,
For roads on earth cannot preserve several layers of prints.
But roads in heaven preserve eternally all layers of prints
All traces of steps.
On our earthly roads there is a single matter, earth,
Our earthly roads are never made of anything but earth,
And it serves all the time, and it can serve only once
At a time
It is the same earth that serves all the time.
It never keeps more than one layer of prints at a time.
In order to receive another it must sacrifice
The preceding layer.   Always the preceding one.
One print effaces another.   A step effaces a step.   A foot-
    print effaces a footprint.
That is why we say we are treading the same road.
It is because this same road is one road, the same road of
    the same earth.
In the same earth.
But the roads of heaven eternally receive imprints,
New imprints,
And he who passes at the eleventh hour along the roads of
    heaven (A certain man had two sons)
To go to his work and he who returns from his work
Plants in the soil a new imprint
    An eternal imprint
Which is his very own print and he leaves forever
Untouched the prints of all those
Who have passed before him.   Who have passed since the first
    hour
And even likewise
Untouched the prints

Of him who passed just before.
It is the very miracle of heaven, the miracle of every day
     in heaven, but on earth
He who follows effaces the prints of him who precedes.
Footprints efface footprints
In the same sand.
He who walks behind effaces the prints of him who walks before.
And when we ourselves tread,
When we start along the same road for the twentieth time,
When twenty times we walk behind ourselves,
We efface the marks of our (own) steps,
Of our former steps.
Yet that is what Jesus did
For thirty years,
Yet in imitation of him it is what Jesus, what God asks
Of those who have not been given
Special public vocations.
And even of others.
Of us who have not been given special vocations,
Extraordinary vocations,
Public vocations,
All our lives.
And even of those who have been given special vocations
Extraordinary vocations,
Public vocations,
During their whole private lives, and even elsewhere, and
     even afterwards
During the thirty years of their private lives, and even at
     other times
For even in public life days are alike.
Starting with the same mornings, leading to the same evenings.
For in every life there are very few days which are not like
     all other days.
But every day counts.   Even in the life of Jesus, even in his
     public life

In his preaching how many days were different.

How many sermons were different and from a temporal view-
point were not repetitions.

There was only one day of the Institution of the Eucharist.
And one day of the Crucifixion.   And one day of the
Resurrection.

(And there will be only one day of Judgment.)

For three and thirty years all the other days were alike.

But every day counts.   For on earth we efface twenty times
our own footprints

And we tread twenty roads all superposed upon the same road.

But in heaven they are not superposed.   They are laid end
to end.   And they form the bridge

That brings us to the other side.

A single road was too short.   A single road.   But twenty end
to end

(Although each of the twenty is the same as the others)

Are long enough.   So when we say that hope deceives us.

And when at the same time in our secret hearts we aid and abet

Her in deceiving us,

In our hearts we know very well what all this means.

And that this secret complicity with her

In deceiving us

Is what there is in us

That is most pleasing to God.

Now she treats us like herself.

As she treats herself.

As if we were like her.

In other words, as if we were tireless.

And she makes us tread twenty times the road.

That is not the same road.

As if we were tireless.

Children do not even think of being tired.

They run like puppies.   They cover the ground twenty times,

And consequently twenty times more ground than necessary.

141

What difference does it make to them.   They know very well
    that in the evening
(But they do not think of it)
They will be ready to drop with sleep
In their beds or even at table
And that sleep is the end of all.
That is their secret, that is the secret of being tireless.
Tireless as children.
Tireless as the child Hope.
And of always beginning again next day.
Children cannot walk, but they know very well how to run.
The child does not even think, does not know that he will
    sleep in the evening.
That in the evening he will fall asleep.   Yet it is this sleep
Always ready, always available, always present,
Always underneath, like a good reservoir,
Yesterday's and tomorrow's, like good food for one's being,
Like a reinforcement of being, like a reservoir of being,
An inexhaustible reservoir.   Always present.
This morning's and this evening's
Sleep that puts strength in his legs.
The previous sleep, the coming sleep
Is this same deep sleep
Continuous as the being itself
That passes from night to night, from one night to the next,
    that continues from one night to another,
By passing above the days
Leaving the days only like eyelets, like openings.
It is this same sleep wherein children bury their being
That keeps for them, that makes for them daily those new legs
Those brand new legs.
And what there is in new legs: new souls.
Those new souls, those fresh souls.
Fresh in the morning, fresh at noon, fresh in the evening.
Fresh as the roses of France.

Those straight-stemmed souls.   That is the secret of being
   tireless.
It is sleeping.   Why do men not make use of it.
I gave this secret to everybody, said God.   I did not sell it.
He who sleeps well, lives well.   He who sleeps, prays.
   (Also he who works, prays.   But there is time for everything.
   And sleep and work
And work and sleep are two brothers.   And they get on very
   well together.
And sleep leads to work and work leads to sleep.
He who works well sleeps well, he who sleeps well works well.)

It must be, said God, that there is an intimacy
That something has occurred
Between this kingdom of France and little Hope.
There is a secret here.   They succeed too well for it to be
   otherwise.   Yet I am told
That there are men who do not sleep.
I do not like the man who does not sleep, said God.
Sleep is the friend of man.
Sleep is the friend of God.
Sleep is perhaps my finest creation.
I myself rested on the seventh day.
He whose heart is pure, sleeps.   And he who sleeps has a pure
   heart.
That is the great secret of being as tireless as a child.
Of having that strength in one's legs that a child has.
Those brand new legs, those new souls,
And of beginning again every morning, always renewed,
Like young Hope, new Hope.
But I am told there are men
Who work well and sleep badly.
Who do not sleep.   What lack of confidence in me.
It is almost more serious than if they worked badly and slept well.

143

Than if they did not work but slept, for laziness
Is not a greater sin than anxiety.
It is even a lesser sin than anxiety
And despair and lack of confidence in me.
I am not speaking, said God, of those men
Who do not work and do not sleep
They are sinners, of course. It serves them right. Great
    sinners. They have only to work
I am speaking of those who work and do not sleep.
I pity them. I am speaking of those who work, and who
In this are keeping my commandment, poor children.
And who on the other hand lack courage, lack confidence, do
    not sleep.
I pity them. I hold it against them. A little. They do not
    trust me.
As an innocent child lies in the arms of his mother they do not lie
Innocently in the arms of my Providence.
They have the courage to work. They have not the courage to
    do nothing.
They have the virtue to work. They have not the virtue to
    do nothing.
To relax. To rest. To sleep.
Poor things, they do not know what is good.
They manage their business very well during the day.
But they do not want to trust its management to me during the
    night.
As though I were incapable of ensuring the management for one
    night.
He who does not sleep is unfaithful to Hope.
And that is the greatest infidelity
Because it is infidelity to the greatest Faith.
Poor children, they conduct their business wisely during the day.
But when evening comes they cannot bring themselves,
They cannot resign themselves to trust its management to my
    wisdom

144

To trust me for the space of one night with the management
And the administration and conduct of their business.
As if I were incapable, perhaps, of looking after it.
Of watching over it.
Of managing and administering and all the rest of it.
I conduct plenty of business, poor people, I govern creation,
    maybe that is not more difficult.
You might not be out much by leaving your business in my hands,
    wise men.
I might be as wise as you.
You might perhaps hand it over to me for the space of one
    night.
For the time you slept
Anyhow
And the next morning you would perhaps not find it too badly
    damaged.
Next morning it might not be any the worse perhaps.
Maybe I am still capable of taking care of it a bit.
    I am speaking of those who work
And who in this keep my commandment.
And who do not sleep, and who in this
Are refusing all the good of my creation,
Sleep, the best thing I have created,
And refusing also my commandment.
Poor children, what ingratitude toward me
To refuse such a good,
Such a fine commandment.
Poor children they are acting on human wisdom.
Human wisdom says: Do not put off until tomorrow
What you can do today.
And I say to you: He who knows how to put things off until
    tomorrow
Is most pleasing to God.
The man who sleeps like a child
Is also he who sleeps like my dear Hope.

And I say to you: Put off until tomorrow
Those cares and troubles that gnaw at you today
And could devour you today.
Put off until tomorrow those sobs that stifle you
When you see today's misfortune.
Those sobs that rise and strangle you.
Put off until tomorrow those tears that suffuse your eyes
And bathe your face.   That stream from your eyes.   Those tears
    that flow.
Because between now and tomorrow I, God, shall perhaps have
    passed your way.
Human wisdom says: Wretched is he who puts off till the morrow.
And I say: Blessed, blessed is he who puts off till the
    morrow.
Blessed is he who puts off.   That is: Blessed is he who hopes.
    And who sleeps.
Wretched is he who stays awake and does not trust me.
What mistrust of me.   Wretched is he who lies awake.
Wretched is he who drags through the evenings and through the
    nights.
Through the drawing in of the evening and the fall of night.
Like a snail's trail on these beautiful forerunners.
My creatures.
Like a slug's trail on these beautiful nightfalls.
My creatures, my creation.
The slow rememberings of daily cares.
The burns, the bites.
The filthy traces of cares, of bitterness and of anxieties.
Of troubles.
The traces of slugs.   On the flowers of my night.
Verily I say unto you that man offends
My dear Hope
Who does not want to trust the management of his life to me,
While he sleeps.
The fool.

Who does not want to trust the management of his night to me.
As if I had not proved myself.
Who does not want to trust the management of one of his nights
    to me.
As if more than one man.
Who had left his business in a very bad state when he went to bed.
Had not found it in a very good state when he got up.
Perhaps because I had passed his way.
Nights follow each other and are linked, and for the
    child nights are continuous and the foundation of
    his very being.
He falls back on them.   They are the very foundation of
    his life.
They are his very being.   Night is the place, night is
    the being wherein he bathes, feeds, is created, is
    formed.
Wherein he fashions his being.
Wherein he recuperates.
Night is the place, night is the being wherein he rests,
    retreats, meditates.
Wherein he comes home.   And he leaves refreshed.   Night
    is my most beautiful creation.
Now why does man not make use of it.   I am told there
    are men who do not sleep at night.
For children and for my young Hope
Night has its true significance.   It is children who
    see and know.   It is my young Hope
Who sees and knows.   What being is.
What this being, night, is.   It is night that is unbroken.
Children know very well.   Children see very well.
And it is the days that are not continuous.   It is the
    days that pierce, that fracture night
And not the nights that interrupt day.
It is the day that disturbs night,
Otherwise night would sleep.

And the solitude, and the silence of night is so
     beautiful and so great
That it surrounds, encircles, envelops the days themselves.
That it forms a majestic border for the days' commotion.
Children are right, my little Hope is right.   All nights
Meet together and join as in a beautiful round, as in
     a beautiful dance,
A dance of nights with linked hands, and the meager days
Make only a procession without linked hands.
Children are right, my little Hope is right.   All nights
Meet together and join above the borders of days, they
     stretch out their hands to each other
Above the days, form a chain and more than a chain,
A round, a dance, nights hold hands
Above the day, from morning to evening,
From the border of morning to the border of evening,
     leaning toward each other.
The night that comes down from the preceding day leans
     backward
The one going up
For the following day
Leans forward
And the two join, join their hands,
Join their silence and their darkness
And their devotion and their majestic solitude
Above the difficult borders
Above the borders of the laboring day.
And all together, holding hands thus,
Overflowing above the borders, wrists linked
To wrists, all the nights, one after another
Together compose night and the days one after another
Together do not compose day.   For they are never anything
     but meager days
That do not hold hands.   Now in the same way that life
On earth

In a general way (if I may say so), is only a passage
    between two borders
An opening between the night before and the night after
An eyelet
Between the night of darkness and the night of light
So, in a small way, each day is only an opening.
An eyelet.
Not only between the night before and the night after.
Between the two borders,
But as children see, as children feel, and my young
    Hope, as children know, an opening
In the night, in one and the same,
In one and the same night
Wherein being is retempered.
In the depths of night.
It is night that is continuous, wherein being is
    retempered, it is night that weaves a long unbroken
    cloth,
An endless unbroken cloth wherein the days are only
    eyelets,
Open only as eyelets are open.
That is, like holes in an eyelet-embroidered cloth.
In open-worked material.
It is night that is my great black wall
Where days open only like windows
With an anxious and wavering
And perhaps a false light.
Where days open only like eyelets.
Where days open only like dormer windows.
For it must not be said that the chain of time
Is an endless chain
Where joint follows joint, where link follows link,
Where equal days and nights follow each other in the
    same chain.
One white link, one black link, night coupled to day,

day coupled to night.

But they are not equal, they have not the same importance
   in this chain.

It is night that is continuous.   It is night that is
   the cloth

Of time, the reservoir of being

And day opens upon it only through wretched windows
   and posterns.

It is day that fractures and day opens upon it

Only through mean lights

On sufferance.*   It is day that splits and the days are
   like islands in the sea.

Like scattered islands that interrupt the sea.

But the sea is unbroken and it is the islands that are
   wrong.

In the same way it is the days that are wrong and
   broken and interrupt night.

But no matter what they do they themselves

Bathe in night.

As the sea is the reservoir of water so night is the
   reservoir of being.

It is the time I have reserved for myself.   No matter what the
   feverish days do,

As in the open sea, in the middle of night, they bathe
   in the depths of night.

It is they that are scattered, it is they that are
   broken.

The days are the Sporades Islands and night is the open sea

Where Saint Paul sailed

And the border that descends from night to day

Is always a rising border,

A steep border and the border that rises from day
   toward night

*Pun in French.

150

Is always a descending border.   In the depths of night.
    O night, my finest invention, my most majestic
        creation of all.
My most beautiful creature.   Creature of the greatest
    Hope.
You furnish the most substance for Hope.
You are the instrument, you are the very substance and
    the abode of Hope.
And also, (and thus), basically the creature of the
    greatest Charity.
For it is you who cradle the whole of Creation
In restoring Sleep.
As one lays a child in his little bed.
As his mother lays him down and tucks him in
And kisses him   (She is not afraid of wakening him,
He sleeps so soundly.)
As his mother tucks him in and laughs and kisses his
    forehead
For pleasure.
And he too laughs in response in his sleep.
Thus, O night, dark-eyed mother, universal mother,
Mother not only of children (that is so easy)
But mother even of men and women, which is so difficult,
It is you, night, who put all Creation to bed
In a bed of a few hours.
(In the meantime.)   In a bed of a few hours
The reflection, the pale reflection, and the promise
    and prior realization of the bed of all the hours.
An anticipated realization.   A promise kept in advance
While awaiting the bed of all the hours.
In which I, the Father, shall lay my creation.
O Night, you are night.   And all those days
    together
Are never day; they are never anything but days.
Isolated days. Those days are never anything but gleams.

Uncertain gleams, and you, night, are my great dark
   light.
I congratulate myself on having made night.   The days
   are islets and islands
That pierce and break up the sea.
But they have to rest in deep sea.
They are compleled to do so.
Just so you, days, are compelled
You have to rest in deep night.
And you night are the deep sea
On which Saint Paul sailed, not that little lake in
   Galilee.
All those days are never anything but limbs,
Cut off limbs.   It is the days that emerge, but they
   have to be anchored in deep water,
In the depths of night.   Night my finest invention
   you calm, you soothe, you give rest
To sore limbs
All out of joint from the day's work.
You calm, you soothe, you give rest
To sore hearts
To bruised bodies, to limbs bruised by labor, to hearts
   bruised by labor
And sorrow and daily cares.
O Night, O my daughter Night, the most religious of
   my daughters
The most devout.
Of all my daughters, of all my creatures, the most
   obedient, the most submissive.
You glorify me in Sleep still more than your Brother,
   the Day, glorifies me in Work.
For in work a man glorifies me only by his work,
And in sleep it is I who glorify myself by the submission
   of man.
And it is surer, I know better how to go about it.

Night, you are for man more nourishing food than bread
 and wine.
For if he who eats and drinks does not sleep, his food
 does him no good.
It will turn sour, and lie heavy on his stomach.
But if he sleeps, bread and wine become his flesh and
 blood.
For working.   For praying.   For sleeping.
Night you alone dress wounds.
Sorrowing hearts.   Broken.   Torn.
O my dark-eyed daughter, you alone of my daughters are
 and can call yourself my partner.
You are my partner, for you and I, I through you
Together we cause man to fall into the snare of my
 arms
And we take him a bit by surprise.
But one takes him as one can.   I ought to know.
Night, you are a fine invention
Of my wisdom.
Night, O my daughter Night O my silent daughter
At Rebecca's well, at the well of the Samaritan woman
You draw the deepest water
From the deepest well.
O night, you cradle all creatures
In restoring sleep.
O night, you bathe all wounds
In the only fresh water, in the only deep water
At Rebecca's well, drawn from the deepest well.
Friend of children, friend and sister of young Hope
O night, you dress all wounds
At the well of the Samaritan woman from the deepest
 well you draw
The deepest prayer.
O night, O my daughter Night, you know how to be silent,
 O my daughter of the beautiful mantle,

153

Who shed rest and forgetfulness. Who shed balm, and
    silence, and darkness
O my starry Night I created you first.
You who put to sleep, who already enshroud in eternal Darkness
All my most anxious
Creatures, the fiery steed, the industrious ant,
And man that monster of anxiety.
Night you succeed in quieting man
That well of anxiety.
More anxious in himself than all creation put together.
Man, that well of anxiety.
Just as you quiet the water in the well.
O my night of the great robe
You gather children and young Hope
Under the folds of your robe
But men resist your help.
O my beautiful night I created you first.
And almost before the first
O silent one of the long veils
With whom descends to earth a fore-taste
Who with your hands shed on earth
An advance peace
        Fore-runner of eternal peace,
And advance rest
        Fore-runner of eternal rest.
An advance balm, so cooling, an advance bliss
        Fore-runner of eternal bliss.
You soothe, you are fragrant, you comfort.
You bind up wounds and bruised limbs.
You put hearts to sleep, you put bodies to sleep
Suffering hearts, suffering bodies,
Aching bodies,
Limbs worn out, backs broken
With weariness, with care, with anxieties,
Mortal anxieties,

With troubles,
You pour balm on throats rent by bitterness
Cooling balm
O my great-hearted daughter I created you first
Almost before the first my great-bosomed daughter
And I well knew what I was doing.
I surely knew what I was doing.
You lay the child in his mother's arms
The child enlightened by a shadow of sleep
Laughing inwardly, laughing secretly because of his confidence
    in his mother.
And in me,
Laughing secretly with a crinkle of his serious lips
You lay the child inwardly replete and brimming with innocence
And confidence
In his mother's arms.
You used to lay the baby Jesus every evening
In the arms of the Very Holy and Immaculate One.
You open the door for hope.
O my daughter, first among all.   You even succeed,
You sometimes succeed
You lay man in the arms of my Providence,
My maternal Providence.
O my daughter, glittering and dark I greet you
You restore, you nourish, you refresh,
O silence of darkness
Just such silence reigned before the creation of anxiety.
Before the beginning of the reign of anxiety.
Such a silence will reign, but it will be a silence of light
When all this anxiety is consumed,
When all this anxiety is exhausted.
When they have drawn all the water from the well.
After the consummation, after the exhaustion of all this anxiety
Of man.
So, daughter, you are ancient and you are late

For in this reign of anxiety you suggest, you commemorate,
   you almost establish again,
You almost bring about a renewal of the former Quietude
When my spirit brooded over the waters.
But also, my starry daughter, my daughter of the dark mantle,
   you are very much ahead of time, you are very early.
For you announce, for you represent, for you almost bring
   about every evening the renewal ahead of time
Of my great Quietude of light,
Of eternal light.
Night you are holy, Night you are great, Night you are beautiful,
Night of the great mantle.
Night I love you and greet you and glorify you and you are my
   big daughter and my creature
O beautiful night, night of the great mantle, my daughter of the
   starry mantle
You remind me, even me, of the great silence there was
Before I had opened the flood-gates of ingratitude.
And you presage for me, even for me, the great silence there
   will be
When I have closed them.
O sweet, O great, O holy; O beautiful night, perhaps the holiest
   of my daughters, night of the great robe, of the starry
   robe
You remind me of the great silence there was in the world
Before the beginning of the reign of man.
You presage for me the great silence there will be
At the end of the reign of man, when I have resumed my scepter.
And I look forward to it sometimes, for truly man makes a lot
   of noise.
But especially, O Night, you remind me of that night,
And I shall remember it forever.
The ninth hour had struck in the country of my people Israel.
It was all over.   That tremendous adventure.
From the sixth hour there had been darkness over all the land
   until the ninth hour.

It was all over.   Let us not talk of that any more.   It pains
   me.
That unbelievable descent of my son among men.
Into the midst of men,
When you think how they reacted.
Those thirty years that he was a carpenter in the midst of men
Those three years that he was a sort of preacher in the midst
   of men.
A priest.
Those three days that he was a victim in the midst of men.
Among men.
Those three nights that he was a corpse in the midst of men.
Among dead men.
Those centuries and centuries that he has been a host in the
   midst of men.
It was all over, the unbelievable adventure
That has tied my hands for all eternity.
The adventure by which my Son has tied my hands.
Eternally tying the hands of my justice, eternally loosing
   the hands of my mercy.
And even inventing a justice opposed to my justice.
A justice of love.   A justice of Hope.   It was all over.
That which was necessary.   As it had to be.   As my prophets had
   foretold it.   The veil of the temple had been rent in
   twain, from top to bottom.
The earth had quaked; rocks had split.
Graves had opened, and several bodies of saints who were dead
   were restored to life.
And about the ninth hour my Son had uttered
The cry that will never fade.   It was all over.   The soldiers
   had returned to their barracks.
Laughing and joking because another task was finished.
One more guard duty they would not have to stand.
Only one centurion remained, and a few men
A very small guard for the unimportant gibbet.

The gallows where my Son was hanging.
Only a few women had remained.
The Mother was there.
And maybe also a few disciples, that is not certain.
Now every man has the right to bury his son
Every man on earth, if he has the great misfortune
Not to die before his son.   And I alone, God,
My hands tied by this adventure,
I, alone, a father at that moment after so many fathers,
I alone was unable to bury my son.
It was then, O night, that you came.
O my daughter dearest of all and I see him still and I shall
   see that throughout eternity
It was then O Night that you came and in a great shroud you
   enveloped
The centurion and his Roman men,
The Virgin and the holy women,
And that mountain and that valley, where the dusk was drawing
   in,
And my people Israel and the sinners, along with him who was
   dying, who had died for them
And the servants of Joseph of Arimathea who were already
   approaching,
Bearing the white grave-cloth.